D0406943

SINCE YOU ASKED

Other books by Marilyn Meberg

I'd Rather Be Laughing
Choosing the Amusing
The Zippered Heart
Assurance for a Lifetime
God at Your Wits' End

SINCE YOU ASKED

Answers to Women's Toughest Questions on

RELATIONSHIPS

MARILYN MEBERG

W PUBLISHING GROUP
A Division of Thomas Nelson Publishers
Since 1798

www.wpublishinggroup.com

© 2006 by W Publishing Group. All rights reserved. No portion of this book may be reproduced, stored in a retrieval system, or transmitted in any form or by any means—electronic, mechanical, photocopy, recording, or any other—except for brief quotation in printed reviews, without the prior permission of the publisher.

Published by W Publishing Group, a division of Thomas Nelson, Inc., P.O. Box 141000, Nashville, TN 37214.

W Publishing books may be purchased in bulk for educational, business, fundraising, or sales promotional use. For information, please email SpecialMarkets@ThomasNelson.com.

All Scripture quotations, unless otherwise indicated, are taken from The New King James Version (NKJV®), copyright 1979, 1980, 1982, Thomas Nelson, Inc., Publishers. Other Scripture quotations are taken from the following: The King James Version of the Bible (KJV). The Message by Eugene H. Peterson (MSG), copyright © 1993, 1994, 1995, 1996, 2000, 2001, 2002. Used by permission of NavPress Publishing Group. All rights reserved. New American Standard Bible (NASB), © 1960, 1977 by the Lockman Foundation. The Holy Bible, New International Version (NIV). Copyright © 1973, 1978, 1984, International Bible Society. Used by permision of Zondervan Bible Publishers. The *Holy Bible*, New Living Translation (NLT), copyright © 1996. Used by permission of Tyndale House Publishers, Inc., Wheaton, Illinois 60189. All rights reserved.

Library of Congress Cataloging-in-Publication Data

Meberg, Marilyn.
    Since you asked: answers to women's toughest questions on relationships / Marilyn Meberg.
    p. cm.
    ISBN 0-8499-0049-2
    1. Christian women—Religious life. 2. Interpersonal relations—Religious aspects—Christianity. 3. Wives—Religious life. I. Title.
    BV4527.M436 2006
    248.8'43—dc22

2005035032

Printed in the United States of America

06 07 08 09 10 QW 9 8 7 6 5 4 3 2 1

DEDICATION

I dedicate this book to my parents, Elizabeth and Jasper Ricker, who watched with amusement as the neighborhood kids started dropping by to "ask marilyn". What my parents found amusing was that I was only 12 years old when it all began. Most of the "drop bys" were teenagers. Once I overheard my father say to my mother "what in the world do you think Marilyn tells them . . . she's just a kid". My mother's response was, "whatever she's saying, they keep coming back". With a twinkle in his eye, dad suggested I could augment my allowance by charging 10 cents a session.

What my parents may not have realized is that from my earliest years, they provided a model for listening and caring as I observed them interact with various church members who "dropped by" for encouragement. And incidently those church members were never charged 10 cents per session.

And so, dear mom and dad, I continue to be flattered when people drop by and ask Marilyn. I also continue to be instructed by my memory of how you were and how you did it.

CONTENTS

Introduction ix

One: The Soar-Wallow Syndrome 1

Two: Transformed Thinking 15

Three: Two Shall Become One 25

Four: Domination and Resistance 37

Five: His Secret Sin. 51

Six: Where Is God? 65

Seven: Meet the In-laws 77

Eight: He Wants Me to Do *What*?. 89

Nine: Looking for Loopholes 101

Intermission 119

Ten: I Want to Start Over 123

Eleven: What About the Kids? 135

Twelve: Facing the Grotesque. 151

Thirteen: Forgiving and Forgetting 167

Fourteen: Managing Our Expectations 179

INTRODUCTION

In 2004, Women of Faith sent out hundreds of surveys to women, asking them to share something very private and personal. What were their struggles? What were their undisclosed pains? What were their points of greatest need? And if they could sit down with counselor and Women of Faith speaker Marilyn Meberg, what would they ask her?

The response was overwhelming, and questions poured in. Women all across the country wrote their "Dear Marilyn" letters. They were willing to draw back the curtain and show Marilyn their secret places. They shared their stories of betrayed confidences, childhood abuses, misspent youths, disappointed expectations, soul-shattering tragedies, and confusion about God's purposes. Each came to the table with questions that are awkward to ask and even harder to answer. "Enough is enough—do I have grounds for divorce?" "What does

God think about my homosexual past?" "How do I deal with my overbearing mother-in-law?" "Can God forgive my son's suicide?" These emotionally charged questions came with heartfelt pleas for sound, biblical advice.

In this first book in the *Since You Asked* series, Marilyn responds to the questions about relationships—questions on separation, divorce, desertion, infidelity, sex, pornography, submission, in-laws, exes, adolescents, remarriage, abuse, forgiveness, homosexuality, and suicide.

Thank you to all the women out there who had the courage to speak up. Since you asked, women across the country now have the chance to find hope and light for the darkest corners of their lives.

ONE

THE SOAR-WALLOW
SYNDROME

> *From the depths of despair, O LORD, I call for
> your help.*
>
> *—Psalm 130:1* NLT

arl Sandburg captured well the human condition:
"There is an eagle in me that wants to soar, and
there is a hippopotamus in me that wants to wallow in
mud." Have we not all been in that state at some point
in our lives? What causes most of us to either soar or
wallow are human relationships. They are capable of
sending us to great heights of fulfillment (the eagle) or
great depths of disappointment (the hippo).

Yesterday, I watched Oprah Winfrey interview a
well-known Hollywood actor. This guy was soaring all
over the place. In fact, apparently unable to contain

himself, he leaped from the couch to the floor, from the floor to the back cushions, and plopped exuberantly back to the seat cushions as he described his latest and best heartthrob to Oprah.

He's never felt more deeply, loved more fully, or experienced greater joy in any relationship. This relationship is what he's been waiting for his entire life. Unfortunately, because he's a public figure, we've seen and read about him soaring and then wallowing in three previous relationships (but of course that was then, and this is now, right?).

> *What causes most of us to either soar or wallow are human relationships. They are capable of sending us to great heights of fulfillment or great depths of disappointment.*

The soar-wallow syndrome is not limited to affairs of the romantic heart. We experience it in friendships as well. Haven't we all glowed with what we assumed was the limitless potential to have our soul needs met by a new friend? That friend's heart seems to beat in synchronized rhythm with ours. Our wishes, goals, spiritual convictions, quirky ways, and rarely shared secrets all find a mutual meeting place as well as a safe haven in hours of conversation. It's what we've been waiting for our entire lives. We are eagles.

Perhaps our greatest hopes for soaring come in anticipation of perpetual wedded bliss. In that relationship we will know unconditional love, unending companionship, and emotional/physical oneness. That nagging feeling of rootless aloneness will be eliminated when we belong to someone.

Last Saturday night, Patsy Clairmont, Lana Bateman, Pat Wenger, and I were heading out for dinner after our Pittsburgh conference. As we walked by the stately First Presbyterian Church, we all stopped with rapt pleasure and attention. Standing on the sidewalk and steps to the church were people in tuxedos and gorgeous long gowns. As we watched, the Cinderella bride and her handsome groom arrived in their midst. Mounting steps that elevated them higher than those around them, they shared a kiss and then released from a gold box two exquisite white doves that soared away into the lavender night. Within seconds, ten more white doves were released, which also soared away. "Ah yes," everyone sighed. "How perfect . . . how lovely." The image of a hippopotamus never crossed our minds. We were not wallowing. We were soaring.

I will never forget the overwhelming tenderness and awe I felt as I stared into the perfectly formed, innocent dimpled face of our baby boy, Jeff. Sorry, God, sorry Ken, but there were moments when I didn't think either of you had anything to do with that baby's beauty. I felt unreasonable personal pride in everything about him. How could it be that my body housed such a vast miracle? What did I—we—do to deserve so rich a blessing?

Some years later, looking into that unflinching face, I wondered how he could lie to me so effortlessly. Who taught him to deny he had four Mystic Mint cookies after school at Tommy Fishbeck's house?

And how could Beth promise not to see *that boy* and then meet him after school at Jiminy Cricket's yogurt shop? Did she think it was okay to deceive us? Is it only wrong if you get caught? Didn't anyone take time to teach these precious ones values? Move over, hippo.

Jeff was six years old when he came to agree with Mark Twain's famous denouncement: "People are no d— good." Jeff was sitting cross-legged on his bed one morning, thumbing through a *Playboy* magazine. (I had no idea what magazine he was thumbing through or where he got it, but that he was enthralled was undeniable. That I was beyond horrified is a subject for another time.)

Later, when I walked by his room, he was playing quietly on the floor with Legos. Following that activity, he started making shapes out of Play-doh.

"Baby, don't you want to go outside and play? I see Tommy Fishbeck is in his front yard by himself. Why don't you invite him over?"

"No, Mama, I'm pretty much done with Tommy Fishbeck."

I decided not to press it and suggested he might want to go next door to Johnnie's house. Miss Mona was home, and I'd take a quick run to the grocery store. Then Jeff could play with Johnnie.

"No, Mama, I'm pretty much done with Johnnie."

"Well honey, how about Nell? She's out riding her bike."

Jeff gave me one of his long-suffering stares and said, "I'm pretty much done with everyone in this neighborhood, and I'm close to being pretty much done with everyone at school, including Mrs. Chopin." (Mrs. Chopin was his teacher, and to my knowledge never composed any music.)

Well, mercy! Serious stuff was going on, so I joined him in making shapes from Play-doh. Jeff filled me in with a litany of personal grievances he'd been experiencing. Tommy kept Jeff's Tonka dump truck and said he didn't have it. Nell was a girl. Johnnie stole a quarter from Jeff, then lied about it and kept the quarter. Mrs. Chopin told Jeff his printing was the worst she ever saw (hearing that made me feel pretty much done with her myself), and he really didn't know anyone who was nice. Sighing deeply, he said he just planned to stay in the house.

"How long do you plan to stay in the house?"

"Maybe 'til I'm forty."

Well, I thought to myself, *this will be a long childhood.*

I love C. S. Lewis's erudite description of the heart-longing we all have for relationships that satisfy our souls and quiet our murmurings. Enjoy the poetic beauty of his words, and see if you agree with his conclusion:

Are not all lifelong friendships born of the moment when at last you meet another human being who has some inkling (but faint and uncertain even in the best) of that something which you were born desiring, and which beneath the flax of other desires and in all the momentary silences between the louder passions, night and day, year by year, from childhood to old age, you are looking for, watching for, listening for? You have never had it. All the things that have ever been but hints of it—tantalizing glimpses, promises never quite fulfilled, echoes that died away just as they caught your ear.

If there ever came an echo that did not die away but swelled into the sound itself—you would know it. You would say, "Here at last is the thing I was made for." We cannot tell each other about it. It is the secret signature of each soul, the incommunicable and unappeasable want, the thing we desired before we met our wives or made our friends or chose our work, and which we shall still desire on our deathbeds.

I interpret Lewis as saying that what we long for is never fully satisfied on this earth. We experience "tantalizing glimpses," but that which we've desired for a lifetime follows us to the end of our lifetimes. I hate to drastically alter the linguistic mood Lewis creates, but it sounds as if the best we can expect on this earth is an occasional soar followed by a prolonged wallow.

That sounds too bleak to satisfy me. Admittedly, our deepest soul-longings are often more primal echo than experiential fulfillment. We understand that truth when we remember the consequences of Eve's disobedience and Adam's witless cooperation in that disobedience— paradise lost. However, I believe we can soar more frequently when we understand God's loving intent for each of our individual lives. With that understanding, we may avoid some time-consuming wallowing. Remember, the soar-wallow syndrome was not in God's original blueprint.

> *I believe we can soar more frequently when we understand God's loving intent for each of our individual lives.*

In addition to a fuller understanding of God's intent, we have the opportunity to discard some life patterns that don't work. We can learn new patterns that have a better success rate. Those new patterns are established by learning new ways of thinking. Romans 12:2 states, "Let God transform you into a new person by changing the way you think" (NLT).

If we think as my little Jeff did—the best way to avoid the pain of people is to avoid people—we need a new "think." We were made for relationships. Relatedness was in the original blueprint. Trying to avoid relationships is going against God's design for you, for me, for all of us. Everything in life is about relationship.

Let's flip back to the beginning of time and remember what God said prior to creating Eve. In Genesis 2:18, we read, "The LORD, God said 'It is not good for the man to be alone. I will make a companion who will help him'" (NLT). It was not at this point that God created Eve. According to Genesis 2:19, God first "formed from the soil every kind of animal and bird. He brought them to Adam to see what he would call them, and Adam chose a name for each one" (NLT). But even a man and his dog were not enough. God said "still there was no companion suitable for him" (Gen. 2:20 NLT).

For those who want to avoid relationships and simply love and adore a pet to the exclusion of a human relationship, God says that's not enough. God is obviously not against loving animals, but they are not a suitable substitute, which is why God created Eve.

Adam was ecstatic! In fact, I'd say he did some soaring! Listen to his words in Genesis 2:23: "'At last!' Adam exclaimed. 'She is part of my own flesh and bone! She will be called "woman" because she was taken out of a man'" (NLT).

This is a sidebar thought, but it gives me a giggle to read Adam's words, "At last!" What in the world did he know about "at last"? He barely knew "at first." What he knew was that he wanted something—he had no way of knowing what—and the minute he saw it, you'd think he'd been crying out for centuries, "I need a woman. At last, at last, here she is!"

What Adam did not know, and many of us don't seem to know even yet, is that we are inherently wired for loving. We are wired for relationships. We all desperately want to be loved. We were created for it. To deny it, fight it, or ignore it is to go contrary to a God-given core instinct. And we need to know this instinct extends beyond male-female relatedness. It includes every human interaction on the planet. God seems to think it's better than a cocker spaniel.

Now, quite frankly, I can think of a number of relationships I'd rather drop off at the Humane Society. Some of those relationships have not been housebroken, and I've had enough. My patience is gone; I want them gone. And besides, I can't afford new carpeting one more time! If perchance those thoughts resonate with you, let me tell you about my neighbor's house. (Well, of course, Marilyn, —what better time to talk about your neighbor's house!)

9

This house is three doors down from me on the other side of the street. I thought it would be a great house for Pat Wenger. It was for sale, it was gorgeous, and it was in the center of our new little Women of Faith hub. Of course, the fact that Pat transcribes all my writing into the computer meant she would be well-located for those many occasions when her technological prowess could pull me out of a wallow. She'd also be well located for those times when the soul longs for patio time munching on pizza and simply loving the Texas skies.

She made a bid on the house, and it was accepted. Everyone in the hub was thrilled. One huge problem: the building inspector found significant structural damage evidenced by huge cracks in the foundation. According to the inspector, it was only a matter of time before the house would be uninhabitable. Appalling! Shocking!

Pat withdrew her offer, got her money back, and we sat on the curb staring in disbelief. Such a gorgeous house—perfect landscaping, inviting little side patio complete with fountain softly gurgling in quiet serenity for those who would never guess the existence of structural damage and potential collapse.

But that's not the end of the story. Since its condemning report, the owners no longer had the option of selling the house. So they hired experts to fix the foundation. For months there was a constant flurry of reconstruction going on down there. Funny-looking little bulldozers scurried about, the lawn was torn up, and the flowers were destroyed. Strange building sounds filled the air.

Now, five months later, the little bulldozers have crawled back onto their truck and been driven away. The lawn has been replaced and the flowers replanted, and everything looks spontaneously renewed. Instead of moving to Florida, as the owners had originally intended, they plan to stay. Their house is declared safe and inhabitable, the fountain gurgles with renewed optimism, and the owners can't imagine why they ever wanted to move in the first place.

But here's the less-than-admirable reality. They wanted to move because they didn't want to face their house problems. Instead, they wanted to escape their house problems—sell the house problems to someone else and make a quick escape to Florida. Didn't work. Had to face the house and fix it! Now they're glad they did, but it was not their first choice. Their first choice was to run and not look back.

Since moving to Frisco, Texas, I've learned that foundational problems here are a continual challenge. One builder told me the ground is not stable enough to support all the sudden building going on in this part of the state. As a result, it is not uncommon for many foundations to have little hairline cracks as the soil settles, searching for stability.

So what does my neighbor's house have to do with the topic of relationships? What does the slightly shifting ground in and around Frisco have to do with whether or not we are tempted to drop a few of our relationships off at the Humane Society? I think the house can serve as a metaphor for all of us as we work our way through the shifting soil of relationships.

> *I believe all soul foundations are fixable, capable of repair, and not hopelessly destined for collapse. The key to that repair is not running away but facing the challenges.*

Quite frankly, if I didn't have a few hairline cracks of my own and certainly a touch of foundational instability, some relationships would not put me in a wallow. If I don't stand up and take a look at those fundamental issues, I'm going to be searching madly for a ticket to Florida.

I believe all soul foundations are fixable, capable of repair, and not hopelessly destined for collapse. The key to that repair is not running away but facing the challenges.

The purpose of this book is to suggest a major scriptural guideline for the repair of your relational foundations. As I mentioned earlier in this chapter, that guideline is found in Romans 12:2: "Let God transform you into a new person by changing the way you think"

(NLT). It is possible to learn new patterns of behaving by thinking about what did not work "last time." Based on what has *not* worked, we can change directions and not fall into the rut of unwise pattern repetition. By the same token, we can remember what *did* work last time and what process brought it about.

Over and above it all is God's promise to be with us as He lovingly leads us into new patterns. The verse does not say "Get your stuff straightened out, baby . . . Don't count on Me to be there while you're working on it . . . You make too many dumb mistakes for Me to hang around and watch . . . You create too much foundational stress . . . I'm going to Florida."

The key phrase is, "Let God transform you." He is vitally, energetically, lovingly orchestrating your trans-formation. You are in partnership with Him in this process. You are not in it alone. However, the word "let" makes it clear what we do to be in this partnership. We choose. We "let" God do what He does best—transform us. My part? Choose to participate.

Two

Transformed Thinking

> Let God transform you into a new person by changing the way you think.
>
> —*Romans 12:2* NLT

Marriage gets a lot of bad press. One cynic said, "Marriage is a lot like the army; everyone complains, but you'd be surprised at the large number that reenlist." That quote reflects our contention that the greatest longing of the human heart is for relatedness. If it doesn't work the first time, reenlist with someone else. Consider the following letter.

> Dear Marilyn,
>
> I am forty-one years old and have been married two times. Each marriage ended in divorce. I

am embarrassed by those failures. I'm also surprised I keep trying. Neither of my husbands cared
much about God but didn't seem to mind that I do.
I'm a Christian and want God's will for my life.
What am I doing wrong? I prayed about both marriages. I really want to raise my three boys in a good
home. Both husbands were unfaithful to me, and
both were physically abusive. I'm sure all this is my
fault. I'm engaged to be married again, but now I'm
scared. We've been living together for a month, and
he already shows a mean streak. He hasn't hit me,
but he yells a lot. My oldest son says he hates my
fiancé. I keep praying, but I don't get any answers.

—Cold Feet

Sweet baby, where are you looking for answers?
What kind of answers do you want? The Bible answers
a question you don't seem to be asking. You should not
be living with your fiancé. You should not be having sex
with him. Why? Read 1 Thessalonians 4:3–5: "God wants
you to be holy, so you should keep clear of all sexual sin.
Then each of you will control your body and live in holi-
ness and honor—not in lustful passion as the pagans do
in their ignorance of God and his ways" (NLT). Just in
case you need additional scriptural support on this subject, read 1 Corinthians 6:18–20:

Run away from sexual sin! No other sin so clearly affects the body as this one does. For sexual immorality is a sin against your own body. Or don't you know that your body is the temple of the Holy Spirit, who lives in you and was given to you by God? You do not belong to yourself, for God bought you with a high price. So you must honor God with your body. (NLT)

Now, honey, those Scriptures are so clear, you don't even need to pray about them. You just need to obey them. They are requirements about how we all are to be living. You say you are a Christian and want God's will for your life. There you have it, baby. I suggest you move out.

Now let's look at an obvious pattern in your marriages. You marry nonbelieving, abusive men. Is that kind of man your only option? Are there no choices here for you? Do those choices work for you? The answers are no, no, and no. Remember, your "body is the temple of the Holy Spirit, who lives in you and was given to you by God." You can't go marrying people who bash the temple of the Holy Spirit. That's a huge no-no. Just as you are to honor the temple by being sexually pure, you are to honor the temple by protecting it from these cavemen types who like to hit, beat, and diminish a woman. You can't allow that. You "honor God with your body."

God wants to transform you by changing the way you think. I'm afraid you think you deserve to be abused. That's why the men you have chosen in your life are all abusers. Somehow, you think that's right for you. That's wrong for you.

Was your father abusive? Did he yell, kick, hit, and scream? My guess is you are continuing to live out what is familiar to you. Abuse is familiar, and even though you may hate it, you continue to choose it. Feels like home. Once again I say to you, "Move out." Figuratively speaking, you are still living at home.

> *Let me tell you what God would have you think about yourself. You are His child. He's crazy about children.*

Let me tell you what God would have you think about yourself. You are His child. He's crazy about children. Jesus, the visible God to us on earth, surrounded Himself with children. When the disciples tried to shush them out of the way so Jesus could do the "important" work, Jesus reprimanded the disciples. Mark 10:13–16 shows us the tenderness of Jesus:

> One day some parents brought their children to Jesus so he could touch them and bless them, but the disciples told them not to bother him. But when

Jesus saw what was happening, he was very displeased with his disciples. He said to them, "Let the children come to me. Don't stop them! For the Kingdom of God belongs to such as these. I assure you, anyone who doesn't have their kind of faith will never get into the Kingdom of God." Then he took the children into his arms and placed his hands on their heads and blessed them. (NLT)

Since God wants to transform you by changing the way you think, let's consider what He wants you to think. He wants you to think that not only are you His dearly loved child, but He loves you with tender compassion. Psalm 103:13–14 reads: "The LORD is like a father to his children, tender and compassionate to those who fear [reverence] him. For he understands how weak we are; he knows we are only dust" (NLT).

Sweet baby, I suggest you close your eyes for a moment. See the image of Jesus blessing the children, tenderly placing His hands on their heads. Then see yourself as one of the children in that group of little

You are loved. You are worthy. You are precious to Him. See the image and say the words until you begin to grasp their transforming truth.

ones surrounding Jesus. Feel His touch on your head. Rest in this image again and again, every day. God wants to transform your thinking. You are loved. You are worthy. You are precious to Him. See the image and say the words until you begin to grasp their transforming truth.

Remind yourself that God is not judging you. "He understands how weak we are; he knows we are only dust." Tell yourself that even in your past weakness, you have been loved, are loved, and always will be loved. He will enable you to change these poor choice patterns. His desire is that you

Partner with God as He teaches you new ways of thinking. Life can be richer and sweeter than you have known it to be.

be able to provide a good home for your family. He adores you; He adores your boys. Read His Word, listen to His voice, and rest in His arms of comfort. "The eternal God is your refuge, and his everlasting arms are under you" (Deut. 33:27 NLT).

Now do what you know you need to do. Partner with God as He teaches you new ways of thinking. Life can be richer and sweeter than you have known it to be.

Since We're Chatting . . .

It has been said that growing old is like being increasingly penalized for a crime you haven't committed. Whether it's growing old or feeling responsible for every wrong thing that happens in life, many of us are toting a load of guilt we haven't earned.

I had a friend from at least 382 years ago who was constantly apologizing for things she had nothing to do with. Here's an illustration. Our junior high graduation was scheduled to be held outside. It rained. My friend was beside herself with regret and apologies. For one thing, to schedule anything outside in the state of Washington is inviting a wild run for tarps and umbrellas. Someone obviously made an administrative blunder, and that's the person who should have been "awash" with regret and apologies, not my neurotic soon-to-graduate little friend. She refused to come into the gym until every bedraggled thirteen-year-old had sloshed his or her way through the door and sat in hastily arranged chairs near an empty stage.

One could assume my hand-wringing classmate was simply compassionate and caring. She put the needs of others ahead of her own needs. Isn't that an admirable quality? I for one liked that quality because I knew she'd never take the last Hershey kiss. But the reality is, her seemingly generous spirit had its origin in not feeling "good enough." In fact, she was so "not good enough" that somehow rainstorms were her fault. She was so "not good enough" that in her mind, any bad thing could somehow be traced to her. When Cold Feet wrote and said, "I'm sure all this is my fault," I can see the same thinking pattern. Whatever is wrong in life, *I've caused it and I must work like crazy to fix it.*

Cold Feet has made some extremely unwise choices, and she needs to take responsibility for those choices and work toward changing some patterns. But her choices reflect her lack of self-esteem and the belief that she does not deserve to be treated with respect and kindness. My junior high school friend's behavior reflects her belief that everything is her fault. Both beliefs spring from the same source; neither woman understands her inheritance of love and value.

How does a person get that way? As you might expect, it goes back to childhood messages. Those messages get taped in the little tape recorder that plays relentlessly in our brains. For example, "I'm not good enough" is first communicated through the senses of the infant. There are no words for that recording, but there are sensory messages that the infant tucks away for the day when there are words.

The first year of life is when the little one comes to feel whether she is good enough. Good enough is communicated by touch and sound. When Mama is impatient and rough and ignores the baby's crying, the infant gets the message, "I'm not good enough to be held, cuddled, or sung to . . . It's got to be me . . . Something is really wrong with me!" The first year of life is when trust of the environment is established. It's when the infant learns it is possible to receive comfort and love and not rejection or abandonment. To routinely leave a baby endlessly crying is to create a sense of fear, abandonment, and worthlessness. Ultimately, that sense of worthlessness grows as the child grows. If the messages continue to be apathetic or negative, the sense of self is, "I'm not good enough, and that's got to be my fault."

Those messages need to be changed. That thinking needs to change. That's why I suggest that dear Cold Feet envision herself among the children Jesus tenderly touched and blessed. She needs to retape the messages in her head. She needs to hear messages that speak to her of her value, her worth, and her many lovable qualities.

And, since we're chatting, here's another pattern that seems to dog our footsteps. We marry the person who originally hurt us (Mom, Dad, or both) in an effort to heal old childhood wounds. In marriage, we re-create the conditions of our upbringing in order to correct what our early pain was. In other words, if Dad hurt me, "I'll marry someone like him, but the one I marry won't be like him after all. He'll be kinder, and gentler. We will be able to talk, and I can express my feelings without being afraid like

I was when I was a kid. The one I marry won't abuse me but will instead love me and value me the way I always longed for."

The irony here is that the abused one all too often seeks out further abuse, because it's all she has known. Even in trying to correct the childhood pattern, she may not trust any other pattern, so she returns to what is predictable and familiar. Understanding this reaction is the first step to changing the pattern and transforming her thinking.

THREE

Two Shall Become One

> As the Scriptures say, "A man leaves his father and mother and is joined to his wife, and the two are united into one."
>
> —*Ephesians 5:31* NLT

Sex is a big deal. The act itself has threatened the stability of entire nations and civilizations through the ages. We all watched the embarrassing consequences of President Clinton's infidelity and its effect on our government. We also watched the embarrassing consequences for his wife and daughter. We've watched prominent Christian leaders succumb to the moral ramifications of immoral sexual choices. They've lost their churches, their reputations, and often their families. So what's the deal with sex? Bette Davis said sex is God's joke on human beings. Her statement is not true, and yet at times it seems sex can become a bad joke instead of a divine gift. It can become a negative force instead of a positive spiritual experience. So what is it about sex that makes it such a big deal? Consider the following letter:

Dear Marilyn,

This is an embarrassing question, but I don't thing I know anyone whose husband has never wanted sex. Is it me? Is it him? Is sex too painful to have to deal with, and should I just forget it?

We had sex one time on our honeymoon. In the ten years we've been married, we have had sex maybe eight times. The clincher in all this is he is the pastor of a large church in our community. Among other topics, he counsels couples having marital problems. He refuses to discuss what he thinks and feels about sex with me, but it's clear the whole thing is unattractive to him. He is a kind, sensitive, gracious man who loves God and wants to serve Him. Miracle of miracles, we have one six-year-old son. My husband is a supportive and caring daddy. No one would guess he is a totally disinterested bed partner.

I don't feel free to see a counselor about this because our community is small. Our doctor and his wife are close personal friends. I struggle with self-esteem issues because of it and now find myself attracted to the man next door. This scares me. I don't want to become a "desperate housewife." What's your take on a man with zero sex interest?

—Untouched

My take on it is something's wrong! You're right in your assumption that a man with limited sex drive is rare. As you may know, it is more common for a woman to be troubled with issues of sexuality. So let's consider some possible explanations for his "zero interest."

We first need to rule out medical reasons. Since you hesitate to bring in the family doctor, you need to consult someone in another city where your husband is not known. Now of course you're saying, "In your dreams, Marilyn. We don't even talk about the 's' word." And I'm sure you're right. He would brush off your concern, and you'd be back to where you started. But you could get the taboo subject brought to light by simply saying you continue to be mystified as well as devastated by the no-sex policy of your marriage. You could say that you are concerned about his physical well-being and want him to have a complete medical workup. Quite frankly, I don't think he'll respond positively to this, and I also question the possibility that his disinterest is for medical reasons. He must have a healthy sperm count to produce a baby during one of the few times you've had sex. Nevertheless, a medical workup is the first order of business, if for no other reason than to rule it out as a problem.

This, too, seems unlikely, but is there any possibility of an old flame whom he still loves and with whom he may share some steamy nights, mornings, or afternoons? Is he managing to lead a double life that no one would suspect? This sounds like a grade D movie, but one never knows for sure. No one would have suspected the good Reverend Dimmesdale in *The Scarlet Letter* was the one responsible for Hester's scarlet A.

Another possibility is a gender challenge. He might have homosexual inclinations that he is horrified by and continually fights. As a result, he turns off all sexual impulses as best he can and does not talk about them or indulge in them. He could effectively counsel people on marital topics because the subject isn't about him. He could distance himself and speak out of head knowledge.

And then, he may be one of those few men who simply have minimal interest in anything sexual. There are a few of them out there, and you may have married one of them. If he is, as you say, a caring father and is a "kind, sensitive, gracious man who loves God," you are put into a difficult position. The greatest challenge in a no-sex marriage is achieving God-ordained, genuine intimacy. The marriage relationship is meant to bring two people together in a mutual expression of oneness—literally.

You know all that and obviously are not experiencing all that. So what do you do to keep yourself from becoming a desperate housewife? Since you probably cannot convince him to get marriage counseling (that would be my preference for you both), I strongly suggest you get counseling on your own. Go to another city if you must, but it's imperative that you have someone to walk you through your mounting anger and feelings of rejection. You will be less likely to have neighborly chats with the man next door if you are dealing with the issues that are driving you to notice the man next door.

Finally, decide in your mind if what you have with your husband is enough for you to survive. There is no doubt you're on starvation rations, but determine if the positives outweigh the negatives. Many women feel trapped in marriages where abuse and cruelty are daily experiences. Not only do they not have soul intimacy that is the result of healthy sex, but they don't have healthy anything. You, on the other hand, have a man who is a good father, loves God, and is kind. I know you crave the physical intimacy we were created for. You also crave and deserve emotional intimacy. Since your husband has distanced himself from all personal intimacy and lives instead behind his "nice face," you are left feeling lonely and betrayed. His nice face almost makes you feel guilty, because how do you criticize someone who is so nice? "There must be something wrong with me," goes the familiar refrain.

I suggest that while seeking a counselor who will coach you through those issues, you do not distance yourself from your husband out of your own frustration. Instead, draw him to you in ways that are safe for him. Ask him about his day and his concerns, and tell him about your day and your concerns as well. You need not live in a verbal vacuum. At least know each other to the degree that it's possible without the sexual nightcap. Then, determine for yourself if this is better than the alternative.

Since We're Chatting . . .

It's difficult to see a pattern of behavior for Untouched since she's writing about the pattern of her husband: Pastor No Sex. But I wonder if she did not have some inkling of his disinterest in sex even before she married him? Often there are clues that sexual intimacy may be a challenge. His kisses are not passionate. His hands do not roam. His breathing remains steady. Did she wonder about that? I also wonder what her father was like. Since we frequently marry one parent or the other, I wonder if her father is emotionally unavailable but sitting behind a face of "nice." Might she be re-creating her childhood environment in the hope of capturing the man behind the nice? Many people spend a lifetime in the quest of getting it right in marriage because it wasn't right in childhood.

If indeed my hunch is correct, counseling will help Untouched come to terms with her questing. It will help her resolve the father issues and relate to Pastor No Sex as an adult and not a child. Her child wants an available daddy. He may never show up. Healing that loss will help her accept what is in the marriage as well as enabling her to make an adult choice—accept what is without sulking, withdrawing, or sneaking next door.

I have another hunch about this couple's patterns, and this time I want to consider those of the husband. It certainly appears obvious that he would not agree with the opening statement in this chapter: "Sex is a big deal." What would he say about sex? He refuses to discuss it. Untouched's assumption for him is that he finds sex "unattractive." We discussed several possible reasons, but let me suggest another possibility. Assuming there are no medical problems, no flaming Hester in the wings, no gender challenge, and no lack of testosterone, there could be other sources. It is possible Pastor No Sex had a guilt-driven mother who passed on to him her disgust of anything sexual. When his father tried to kiss his mother, she pulled away and scurried for the kitchen, where she madly stirred the soup. Although they shared a bedroom, his parents each had a twin bed and separate bathrooms. When his sixteen-year-old sister became pregnant, she

31

was sent to another state until the baby was born and given up for adoption. Her pregnancy was never mentioned and the baby never acknowledged. These are powerfully negative messages about sex unconsciously taped in the brain of the future Pastor No Sex. If indeed the pastor picked up his mother's aversion to all things sexual, counseling would help him unearth those buried feelings and come to terms with them. In the process, he might find that he has always longed to love and caress his wife. In the past, yielding to this longing only brought thoughts of guilt and accusation from his distant memory bank and childhood tape recorder.

I would love to think this pastor could one day have his thinking transformed. I would love it if he could one day step into the pulpit and shout, "Sex is a big deal!" Can't you just see the church scene if he did? We'd have a bunch of "tsk-tskers" streaming for the doors in an effort to cleanse their ears and minds before they fell prey to evil. Were I in that congregation during such a moment, I'd clap—maybe shout, "Amen"—but I'd undoubtedly be in the minority (unless Adam was there).

What would you do? What would you say if asked, "Do you think sex is a big deal?" You might be uncomfortable with the pastor shouting that statement as an opener to his sermon, but what do you really think about sex? Let's chat about this subject that seems to embarrass so many and alienate others.

You will remember that the sight of Eve caused Adam to soar with gratitude and ecstasy. When the two virgins experienced each other in all the innocence of a world without sin, they understood with God-given insight, "This explains why a man leaves his father and mother and is joined to his wife, and the two are united into one. Now, although Adam and his wife were both naked, neither of them felt any shame" (Gen. 2:24–25 NLT).

These verses explain why the drive for sexual expression is so strong. The two came from one. They desired to take their separateness and fuse it in a loving act of joining God made two out of one, and each wants to be one again. It's coming home. It's the place where each began and where each longs to return.

Proverbs 30:18–19 expresses the mystery, the majesty, and the beauty of human sexuality, which is God's great gift to all His creation. In wonder, Solomon writes: "There are three things that amaze me—no, four things I do not understand: how an eagle glides through the sky, how a snake slithers on a rock, how a ship navigates the ocean, how a man loves a woman" (NLT). The concept of a man and a woman loving each other transcends the majesty of an eagle soaring through the sky, the odd wonder of a snake on a rock, or a ship moving powerfully through the high seas. Paul makes reference to this God-spoken union of a man and a woman. "As the Scriptures say, 'A man leaves his father and mother and is joined to his wife, and the two are united into one.' This is a great mystery, but it is an illustration of the way Christ and the church are one" (Eph. 5:31–32 NLT).

So, then, how did the original intent and beauty of God-inspired sex go so wrong? Why is sex the source of so much pain, so much misunderstanding, and so much disgusting perversion? You got it—disobedience by the very ones created for unending joyful expression. Adam and Eve ruined it for all of us. Enough was not enough— they wanted more. They got more. They were evicted from Paradise, and they took us with them.

But now wait a minute. Was *everything* totally ruined after the eviction? No. Sex was and continues to be God's gift to creation. But now there's a little something wrong with everything. For example, after the eviction, we read in Genesis 3:16, "I will greatly multiply your sorrow and your conception; in pain you shall bring forth children; your desire shall be for your husband, and he shall rule over you." If it weren't for Eve, we wouldn't need Demerol.

There is a clarifying point to be made about the phrase "your desire shall be for your husband." I have heard that phrase used to support the idea that a woman's sexual desire is a result of that first sin in the garden. That doesn't make sense, since sexual desire was alive and well the minute the two laid eyes on each other. The sins of sex came after sin was introduced. However,

God promises His protection, and He promises to honor the heart that seeks His. We may have been evicted, but we need not be lost. God can help us find our way to our spouses, to enjoy what was originally pure, what is still meaningful and God-created.

FOUR

DOMINATION
AND RESISTANCE

> *You wives will submit to your husbands as you do*
> *to the Lord. For a husband is the head of his wife*
> *as Christ is the head of his body, the church.*
>
> *—Ephesians 5:22–23* NLT

An enthusiastic door-to-door vacuum salesman goes to the first house in his new territory. He knocks, and a mean, tough-looking lady opens the door. Before she has a chance to say anything, he runs inside and dumps cow patties all over the carpet. He says, "Lady, if this vacuum cleaner don't do wonders cleaning this up, I'll eat every chunk of it." She turns to him with a smirk and says, "You want ketchup on that?" The salesman says, "What are you talking about?" She responds with, "We just moved in. There's no electricity until tomorrow."

Now let's do a brief study of this vacuum salesman. To begin with, he did not get permission to invade her space. He simply barged into her home uninvited. He never considered how rude and socially unacceptable his methods are. He's more interested in demonstrating a surefire way to solve the problem he created. What is his number one goal? To manipulate a sale, and at any cost. When he sees his goal is beyond achievement, he has to concede power to the "mean, tough-looking lady." She smirks in triumph.

Could we stretch this fairly bad joke into an illustration? Could we say it's a commentary on the age-old battle between the sexes? The male effort to dominate; the female delight in resisting? Or should we just excuse this author's need for a giggle? Maybe a bit of both is true, but bear with me here.

Would we find the joke funny if the vacuum salesperson were a woman? It would still have some humor, because the salesperson created a ridiculous situation. But doesn't the joke carry the "You deserved that, big guy" sting because it's a man trying to force a sale on a woman? Aren't we rather pleased at the turning of the tables on him? Whether she gave him ketchup or even offered to dash off for steak sauce, she wins and he loses.

Or what if the housewife were not a "mean, tough-looking" lady? What if she were instead a person who lived by a principle of submission to men? She heard it from her father and saw it lived out through the example of her mother.

Consistent with that point of view, what if she apologized to the salesman about not arranging to have the electricity turned on earlier, saying that in essence the whole cow pattie thing was her fault? What if she made him a cup of coffee and then insisted she would have the whole mess cleaned up in a jiffy? He could just sit and relax with his coffee. In fact, he could tell her all about his favorite sports team and why he thinks its coach is brainless, has no class, and should be fired.

How far-fetched is this last scenario? It sounds absurd, and yet there are scores of women who truly believe their role in life is to serve the needs of men at any cost. In fact, in many cultures, women are second-class citizens with no function or importance other than providing for the domestic needs of the household.

Jesus did more for the rights of women than anyone who ever walked the face of this planet.

This morning, I read about Laleh Seddigh, a twenty-eight-year-old race car driver who is the Iranian version of Danica Patrick. Seddigh wears bright pink veils and designer sunglasses and has won a race or two on Iran's racing circuit. State television has refused to broadcast her standing on the podium to receive her prize, but great strides have been made to allow women recognition in a culture known for its female suppression. Seddigh says that because women are now pursuing their rights in ways unthinkable ten years ago, she believes there is reason to hope for cultural change.

Jesus did more for the rights of women than anyone who ever walked the face of this planet. He was consistently concerned with preserving the dignity of women. Even one caught in the act of adultery was lifted from the dirt and dust where her accusers had thrown her. Jesus gently admonished her to "go and sin no more" (John 8:11). Jesus allowed women to travel with Him and the disciples. Together they sought to spread the good news of Jesus and His intent to die for the sins of the world, which would bring forgiveness and salvation to all people.

The morning of the resurrection, it was to a woman the "He is risen" message was given. Women, who had no right to speak in a court of law, were stunned that a woman was the first witness of Jesus' rising from the dead. It was a woman who gave her witness to Peter and John. God could have ordained that earth-shaking message to be placed in the mouth of a man, but He didn't. That place of historical honor was given to a woman. Unheard of . . . unprecedented!

We've come a long way, baby—at least in our

American culture. Women are lawyers, judges, doctors, professors, teachers, nurses, and business executives. Though there is still gender grumbling, the freedoms women enjoy in this culture are gratifying and ever expanding.

That being the case, why is the domination of women an issue in so many Christian circles? Wouldn't one assume that since Jesus was a liberator of women, the very faith that claims His name would also be a liberator of women? There seems to be enormous confusion on the issue of women and their mandatory submission to men. Consider the following question:

Dear Marilyn,

Many of the women who contact our ministry are very confused about submission to ungodly or abusive husbands. Many of them are being told by their pastors that they must submit even if their husbands physically, verbally, or emotionally abuse them, because the husband is the head of the wife. They are told that they will receive God's favor by being a submissive wife, which is their cross to bear. What do you advise a woman to do if the "head [of the household]" is sick?

—Deeply Concerned

Any husband who physically, verbally, or emotionally abuses his wife is totally out of line with the scriptural mandate we read in Ephesians 5:

> You husbands must love your wives with the same love Christ showed the church . . . husbands ought to love their wives as they love their own bodies. For a man is actually loving himself when he loves his wife. No one hates his own body but lovingly cares for it. (vv. 25, 28–29 NLT)

There is no way Scripture supports abuse. How plain can this passage be? "Love your wife as Christ loved the church" leaves no wiggle room for the abusive husband. Christ gave Himself for the church. He sacrificed His life for the church. That is how the husband is to love his wife! Abusive behavior isn't a cross women are called to bear; it is a sin. Better 'fess up, you abusive caveman. You can be forgiven.

While that point is clear, let's consider a more personal letter on the same subject.

Dear Marilyn,

Sometimes husbands, Christian or non-Christian, are not the kind, gentle men we would like them to be. Here's my question. When a husband is frequently cruel and is cutting his wife with

his words, does she stay and live the life of a
Christian woman as an example of Christ to him?
Or, after a long period of trying to bring about change
unsuccessfully, through just about any possible way,
does she leave, since this is a form of abuse? I'm not
sure where the line is, but emotional and mental
abuse is real, although there are schools of thought
among Christian women that you never give up on
your marriage for something like that.

—Wounded

This question is in essence asking, "How much do I
have to take, and for how long?" I think that depends on
the severity of your circumstances. If you or your children are not safe, leave. You must protect your children.
If personal safety is not an issue in your marriage, you
may not have grounds for divorce. However, you may
decide you have adequate reasons for separation. Cruel
and cutting words are demoralizing. Your husband has
no right to speak to you or anyone else in that way.
Separation may shock him into realizing that he has
crossed a personal self-respect boundary and that you
will no longer allow that.

The value of separation is that it provides a time-out
to think about the relationship. It is not a time to
rehearse your grievances—you already know them.
Instead, separation provides a time to evaluate your own

behavior. Ask questions like, "Is there a pattern going on here? Does this look like my childhood home? Are my patterns like my mom's or dad's? Am I repeating a pattern that never has worked, and I just haven't recognized it before?"

During a separation, therapy should occur with a professional, a pastor, or a group to whom you are accountable. Now is the time to grow and evaluate. You may find during this time-out that you have issues of your own that you've never faced before. In other words, shine a light into the dark corners of your own soul. What you learn may change the way you think about your husband, or what you think about yourself in the marriage. I can certainly understand why you'd simply like to give up on the relationship—that's the easier way. I suggest you *not* choose the easier way.

> *Shine a light into the dark corners of your own soul. What you learn may change the way you think about your husband, or what you think about yourself.*

Since We're Chatting . . .

Here's an illustration that just might help us understand this subject better.

A cat shows up at the pearly gates of heaven.

St. Peter: I know you! You were a very nice cat on earth and didn't cause any trouble, so I want to offer a gift to you of one special thing you have always wanted.

Cat: Well, I did always long to own a nice satin pillow like my master had, so I could lie on it.

St. Peter: That's easy. Granted. You shall have the satin pillow after you enter in.

Next a group of mice appear.

St. Peter: Ah, I remember you! You were such good mice on earth. You didn't steal food from anyone's house and never hurt other animals. Therefore, I want to grant you one special wish you always wanted.

The Chief Mouse: Well, we always watched the children playing and saw them roller-skate. It was beautiful, and it looked like so much fun. So can we each have some roller skates, please?

St. Peter: Granted. You shall have your wish.

The next day, St. Peter is making rounds inside the gates and sees the cat.

St. Peter: Well, Cat, did you enjoy the satin pillow?

Cat: Oh, indeed I did. And say, that Meals-on-Wheels
    thing was a nice touch too!

I love satin pillows—they are soft, smooth, and luxu-
rious rewards. Rewards for what? For the cat, for making
it to heaven. For me, just for being alive. I have three huge
satin pillows on my bed that please me enormously. I walk
through the bedroom during the day and look over at
them as they smile regally back at me. Just exchanging
looks with them never fails to smooth my soul.

I suppose they are impractical, as I only use them for
decoration. To haul them onto the floor for a quick sit or
teensy lounge is unthinkable to me. It's just not an option.
Why? I think it's because I sometimes suffer from the
"save-it-for-later" syndrome. Maybe later I won't be so
picky, or maybe later they won't look quite so gorgeous,
or maybe later I could risk getting body lotion on one of
them. In spite of being a confirmed "now" person, I occasionally have little lapses that don't make sense—like sav-
ing my satin pillows for . . . who knows when!

What I'm about to say will probably give you
whiplash, but I'm going to risk your neck and say it anyway. I think the experience of God-ordained marital submission could be a satin pillow for you. If your husband is
conscientiously seeking God's sufficiency in his own life
and thus in yours, you can start to relax. You can start to
feel secure and cared for. That's God's planned pattern for

you. Stretch out on a satin pillow and know your needs are known and cared about.

Now, of course, the Proverbs 31 woman (who can make us all a little tight jawed) did not spend her days lolling around on a pillow. She worked like a Trojan and was praised for doing so. But if God's pattern was accepted in her life, she was on that pillow—perhaps not literally but figuratively. Her soul was smoothed on her satin reward. She was working and accomplishing, but she knew she was loved and honored. Being loved

> *The experience of God-ordained marital submission could be a satin pillow for you.*

and honored is the pillow part. You may be excessively busy, or you may be sitting with tea and pound cake. In any case, your soul needs smoothing. Receiving God's pattern for your marriage is a great reward. Don't save it for later.

Having said that, I once had a male client who loved the phrase "Wives, submit to your husbands in everything." Because it was straight from the Bible, he assumed the command gave him the scriptural right to dominate his wife. God ultimately transformed his thinking, but it was a long process. Common sense tells us that we don't submit in *everything* if the "everything" is contrary to scriptural truth. Abuse is contrary to scriptural truth. We are not required to submit to it. Why? Because the husband is to love his wife as Christ loves the church.

What does that relationship look like? How does the husband's love for his wife look, viewed through the lens of God's pattern for marriage? God's instructions to husbands might sound something like this:

1. You are to love your wife unconditionally.
2. When she makes a mistake and seeks your understanding and forgiveness, you are to immediately forgive her.
3. You can never remind her of her mistakes. You are to forget them; remember them no more.
4. You can never abandon her or betray her.
5. You are to be a husband upon whom she can depend. You are to be strong, wise, and tender.
6. You must always listen to her. Know her heart and listen to her concerns.
7. You must make financial decisions that ensure her security and safety.
8. You must avoid all addictive behavior, including pornography, alcoholism, or drug abuse. You must lead her away from all impurity.
9. You must love her with such commitment and intensity that you would be willing to die for her.
10. You must constantly remind her that she is a treasure.

Amazingly, this list does not cover the many ways Christ loves the church. Who could possibly resist this monolithic love? That is God's pattern for marriage—irresistible love and submissive acceptance. I don't fight the relationship; I receive it. Quite frankly, I can't imagine any woman not choosing to receive such love. It's what we were created for; it's our deepest craving.

"So" we say, "it's what we crave, it's irresistible, but it isn't going to happen. The pattern unraveled. It doesn't fit. The sin thing pulled too many threads to even leave a visible image." That's true. The beyond-Eden world can lose sight of the pattern and settle into disharmony and a determination to have things "my way." Men can dismiss God's call

> *That is God's pattern for marriage—irresistible love and submissive acceptance.*

to biblical headship, which can lead women to a submission that is totally out of touch with reality. Jesus was perfect; husbands and wives are not. So what do we do with God's pattern? To give up on the pattern would be to wallow. God's intent, in spite of Eden, is that we soar.

As in all things too great for our successful accomplishment, in faith, we humbly turn to God and pray for the enablement He promises to provide. Munch and then swallow these words from Romans 10:

Say the welcoming word to God—"Jesus is my Master"—embracing, body and soul, God's work of doing in us what he did in raising Jesus from the dead. That's it. You're not "doing" anything; you're simply calling out to God, trusting him to do it for you ... Scripture reassures us, "No one who trusts God like this—heart and soul—will ever regret it." (vv. 9, 11 MSG).

We trust Him to do in us what we can't. We don't give up; we reach out. God is always there.

FIVE

HIS SECRET SIN

> *Be careful! Watch out for attacks from the Devil, your great enemy. He prowls around like a roaring lion, looking for some victim to devour. Take a firm stand against him, and be strong in your faith.*
>
> *—1 Peter 5:8–9 NLT*

B ased on the preceding chapter, what might you say to the writer of the following letter?

Dear Marilyn,

   Most of my life I have been a single mom. I remarried four years ago and try to be a godly wife, allowing my husband to be the spiritual leader of our home. We each had two children from previous marriages and have one together. My husband claims to be a Christian and attends church, but he admits he rarely prays and doesn't read the Bible. His business dealings are often dishonest, and some of his morals, or lack thereof, are being learned and copied by our children. I have a difficult time keeping quiet about his dishonesty but do so because I do not wish to criticize him in front of our church family. I am starting a new ministry for young adults, and many church leaders are pressuring me to have him be my assistant (he is already a sub for the toddler class). I try to shield my children from his dishonesty (and usually am successful), but I know that he should not hold a position in the church. Not only are some of his dealings dishonest, but they are illegal. I am torn between my loyalty to my husband and trying to be a godly wife, and my duty to the church in shielding others from his dishonesty. Nobody sees it. He is very popular—the life of the party—and I don't wish to bash him at church. Please, any help would be appreciated.

—Keeping Up
Appearances

Okay, darlin', let me be sure I have this straight. You "allow" your husband "to be the spiritual leader" of your home. The description you give of his "leadership" is:

- He rarely prays.
- He does not read the Bible.
- He's dishonest in his business dealings even to the point of being illegal.
- His life is a total sham, and he looks to you to cover for him and make him look good.

You, on the other hand, scramble to divert attention so others do not see who he truly is. And you do this because you want to be a godly wife. Mercy!

I think we need to talk a bit more about wifely submission in marriage. Paul writes in Colossians 3:18, "Wives, submit to your own husbands, as is fitting in the Lord" (NKJV). The pattern for marriage is that the husband is "fit" to head. He must love his wife as Christ loves the church. He must also love with godly integrity. That means the husband seeks a deeper, closer, and more meaningful relationship with God. From that divine relationship, the husband is equipped to be a leader—a leader a wife can trust.

I'm sorry, baby, but your husband fails on all counts. He is not fit to be the leader

> *The pattern for marriage is that the husband is "fit to head." He must love his wife as Christ loves the church.*

of your home. So what does that mean for you, who want to honor him in a position for which he has no qualifications? And what does that say about the degree to which you are to be submissive to him?

Notice the phrase "as is fitting in the Lord" (Col. 3:18). This means that the principle of submission is of the Lord, but it goes beyond that. It means you are not to submit to this husband when he does not follow the Lord. Wives are not under obligation to follow a husband in sin or to quietly condone that sin in the name of marital submission.

You must keep in mind that your first duty is not to be submissive to your husband but to the Lord. Sin can lead a husband to disregard his spiritual role as head. When that happens, you must remember that God has a prior claim on your obedience. Your husband has gone against the divine pattern.

> *Wives are not under obligation to follow a husband in sin or to quietly condone that sin in the name of marital submission.*

One who refused to submit to her husband's sinful demand was Queen Vashti. We read her dramatic story in the book of Esther. Her husband, Xerxes, reigned sometime around 486 BC as a Persian king. His sumptuous consumption of all things extravagant is well documented in history. During one of his hugely elaborate parties that went on for days, the king asked his wife, Queen Vashti, to come to the party and dance for the totally drunk men in attendance. Vashti was gorgeous. King Xerxes was licentiously proud of her beauty and wanted to show her off. She refused to come. King Xerxes was furious. A woman was never to refuse her husband. But Queen Vashti did. As a result, she was stripped of her title, court approval, and personal freedom. Obviously, Vashti's standard for personal purity came before her desire to be queen or to be submissive to her husband. She stood by a spiritual principle that her husband ignored. I admire her.

I remember the indignation of a husband I once counseled. He wanted to use pornography to "spice things up a bit" preceding sex. (Yes, he was a Christian.) The husband found the idea exciting. The wife found the idea offensive. Ultimately, when they couldn't seem to agree, the husband stated, "I'm head of this marriage, and what I say goes!" I was delighted to hear her say, "What goes here is *me* if you insist on using filth to get yourself revved up for sex."

Perhaps one of the reasons the concept of submission gets such bad press is that women think they have to slavishly submit, even when the head is sick. The slogan "No matter what, you must be submissive to the will of the husband" is not true. That is not God's pattern for marriage. We need never mindlessly follow along with demands that are ungodly.

Let's go back now to Keeping Up Appearances' question of what to do with this fun-loving party boy whom everyone enjoys and no one suspects. I find myself wondering what in the world you, dear one, are doing and why you are doing it. Here's my understanding:

- You continually shield him from church scrutiny, knowing he is dishonest.
- You "shield" his behavior from the children, even though they're beginning to imitate him.
- You are starting a ministry for young adults, and though you're being pressured to use him as an assistant, you "know he should not hold a position in the church."
- You say you are "torn" between your loyalty to your husband, "trying to be a godly wife" and trying to keep the church from finding out he's a crook.

Has it occurred to you that you are participating in his dishonesty? Your efforts to keep everyone from finding out that this man lacks character and integrity enable him to continue his deception. Why are you willing to participate in all these cover-ups? Are you afraid you will end up as a single mom again, only now instead of two children, you'll have five? I certainly agree single-ness may not be a pleasant thought, but what price are you willing to pay in your own character and integrity? When all the kids finally get the picture, what kind of example will you be to them? How will you cover that up? What kind of example are you going to be to the young adults you are going to lead and for whom you are to be an example?

Assuming you want God to transform your life by changing the way you think, you have some major rethinking to do. Second Corinthians 6:14 pulls no punches: "Don't team up with those who are unbeliev-ers. How can goodness be a partner with wickedness? How can light live with darkness?" (NLT). Tend to this soon, sweetheart; you may not have a lot of time.

The following questioner is also struggling with a spouse whose secret sin is affecting their children.

Dear Marilyn,

    I fell in love and married the "golden boy" of our small Christian college. He felt God's call to the min-istry. I was thrilled to be a pastor's wife. Five years ago, I discovered his constant use of online pornog-raphy. He begged for my support. A part of that sup-port was to keep his dirty secret. He promised to stop; he hasn't. Now I've discovered that our fourteen-year-old son is also doing online porn. Do I pretend not to know all this? I feel so betrayed. I've lost all respect for my husband, and I'm heartsick his influence may have led to my son's pornography use. I want to run from this. I want a divorce, but what do I do about my son?

—Shocked

Baby, I am so sorry. You must feel as if you've been broadsided by a cement truck. What breaks the heart is not only your husband's deception, but your son's need for immediate help. For that reason, I suggest you not divorce. You may ultimately find your husband's immorality sufficient grounds for divorce, but not yet. Your son needs you, and he requires as much stability in his home environment as you can provide. But first, let's tackle your husband's addiction to pornography.

Your question, "Do I pretend not to know all this?" is understandable, because we all tend to want to deny a problem exists. This difficulty is so enormous that it's hard to know where to begin. We think maybe it will take care of itself and go away. The agony of your husband's situation is that he is a sexual addict. He is addicted to pornography in the same way a drug user is addicted to crack. The two words we use for the addict are "habitual" and "compulsive." His habit must be habitually and compulsively fed. The craving is never ending. Your "golden boy" is gripped by an insidious appetite that I'm sure is causing him personal agony and desperation. So what do you do? You cannot ignore it. You cannot hope it will somehow go away by itself. You must join a fight against all that seeks to destroy the two of you. Before we talk about some clinical approaches I recommend, let me first remind you of the spiritual enemy who daily comes against our souls. First Peter 5:8–9 describes him:

> Be careful! Watch out for attacks from the Devil, your great enemy. He prowls around like a roaring lion, looking for some victim to devour. Take a firm stand against him, and be strong in your faith (NLT).

Satan's greatest tool to use against humankind is sexual perversion and pornography. Its grip is from the pit of hell. So, dear one, you will need to suit up for the battle ahead of you. Psalm 24:8 reminds us whom we are to trust, "The LORD, strong and mighty, the LORD, invincible in battle" (NLT). You do not fight without the power of God, and against Him, no one stands. So then, armed with that biblical truth, what do you do?

> *Satan's greatest tool to use against humankind is sexual perversion and pornography. Its grip is from the pit of hell.*

You must confront your husband with what you know about his Internet pornography patterns. Collect specific data so you can support your findings. Your intent is not to condemn or even accuse. Your intent is to present the facts. In presenting the facts, your husband will have to make some choices. He may become angry that you have dared to "snoop around" for information that you use against him. He may choose to deny your findings. He may lie and say he only goes on the Internet on rare occasions. He may say pornography is not a problem—every man on occasion reverts to pornography. He may say he only uses pornography because you don't fully satisfy him. That last one is an invitation to either run him over with a lawn mower or lace his coffee with strychnine. I hope you have enough feistiness to be tempted but not to yield to either. My concern is that you not buy into his weak blame game. His pornography has nothing whatever to do with you. It is his sickness, and you did not give it to him.

Be prepared for any number of attempts your husband may use to avoid taking responsibility for his addiction. Also be prepared to tell him that if he does not face and then address his problem, you will have no choice but to leave him. That is a perfectly legitimate threat for you to use. You may also say his addiction is being played out in the life of your son and that you have no intention of standing by while those you love are being increasingly diseased. After you have presented your facts and made your ultimatum clear, tell him of a number of treatment options you have researched. Insist he agree to treatment.

If your husband chooses to seek help, it is his huge responsibility to come alongside your son and be an example of one who has confessed his sin and now is attempting to grow from and understand his sin. Your husband's example is crucial for your son's healing. He, too, needs to experience one-on-one therapy for his own issue of sexual addiction. You may ultimately all enter into family counseling together. Each family has a unique dynamic that one needs to recognize in its wholeness to understand what happened and why.

And now, dear one, I'll tell you something you probably already know. It would be best for your husband to resign his pastorate. At least in seeking treatment, he can be a good witness of one who is not hiding in the darkness. You will probably endure the isolating judgment of others. Pastors are held to a higher standard, and when they fall, there are some who fall with them, claiming that all Christians are hypocrites. Some will take the opportunity to blame the Christian leader for their own sin. But be strong in the Lord, sweetheart, and remember that "He who is in you is greater than he who is in the world" (1 John 4:4).

Since We're Chatting . . .

What are some treatment options for sexual addiction? First, you need to find a therapist who is trained and experienced in treating issues of sexual addiction. My preference for you is that you find someone not only skilled professionally, but someone also knowledgeable about Scripture, the role of the Holy Spirit, and the stand-by-you-always support of God's love. Though a pastor has training for your spiritual need, most pastors are not trained to counsel on the level of sexual addiction.

Next, find a treatment center near you. There are many worthy organizations. Here are a few possibilities:

Faithful and True Ministries, Inc.
P.O. Box 84
Chanhassen, MN 55317
(952) 903-9208

L.I.F.E. Ministries
P.O. Box 952317
Lake Mary, FL 32795
(407) 647-9560

National Association for Christian Recovery
P.O. Box 215
Brea, CA 92822
(714) 529-6227

The Meadows
1655 N. Tegner
Wickenburg, AZ 85390
800-MEADOWS or (928) 684-3926

I also strongly recommend 12-step groups for addicts, though not in place of one-on-one therapy with a professional. Twelve-step groups are great for the support and maintenance of what will be learned in therapy. They are an adjunct to therapy. Here are some 12-step group addresses:

Sexaholics Anonymous
P.O. Box 11910
Nashville, TN 37222
(615) 331-6230

Sex Addicts Anonymous
P.O. Box 70949
Houston, TX 77270
(713) 869-4902

Sex and Love Addicts Anonymous
P.O. Box 338
Norwood, MA 02062
(781) 255-8825

SIX

WHERE IS GOD?

> *I know, LORD, that a person's life is not his own.*
> *No one is able to plan his own course.*
> *—Jeremiah 10:23 NLT*

What are we supposed to do with feelings that will not go away and longings that cannot be satisfied? Where is God when we need Him to change things? Let's consider the questions that are brought up in this letter.

Dear Marilyn,

I am forty-one years old (yikes) and have never been married. My desire to have a husband is stronger than any other desire I have ever had. My longing to be intimate with a man is very strong. But the Lord hasn't sent the right man my way—yet.

I do not believe that I was created to live alone for the rest of my life, yet I am alone. The Lord has created within me very strong sexual desires that I have not been successful in keeping in check. I have failed miserably in that arena. However, the Lord has not taken those desires away from me.

Is this a test? Am I supposed to be "perfectly" obedient before He will reward me? Am I supposed to remain single the rest of my miserable life? Or is it just "not my *time* yet"?

I have been asking these questions of the Lord for years. I don't think there really is an answer to this.

—Miserable

What are we supposed to do with feelings that will not go away and longings that cannot be satisfied? Where is God in it all? These are understandable and common questions, yet the answer is simple. The problem is that many of us don't like the answer. So what is the answer? God is sovereign, which means He rules. Psalm 115:3 says, "For our God is in the heavens, and he does as he wishes"

> *What are we supposed to do with feelings that will not go away and longings that cannot be satisfied? Where is God in it all?*

(NLT). Jeremiah 10:23 says, "I know, LORD, that a person's life is not his own. No one is able to plan his own course" (NLT).

You say, "I do not believe that I was created to live alone for the rest of my life." How do you know that? You are assuming that because you want to be married, it must be God's plan for you to be married. Baby, it might not be God's plan for you to marry. That isn't a cruel action on God's part. It is, at least for now, a sovereign action on His part. The crucial question is of course, are you willing to accept His sovereign action?

You say, "The Lord has created within me very strong sexual desires." Then you say you have not been successful in "keeping them in check" and that you have "failed miserably in that arena." And then, as if you're blaming God for your indiscretions, you say, "The Lord has not taken those desires away from me."

Now is the time to present your body to God as a living sacrifice. You are not your own; you've been bought with a price. I know this sounds cranky, but you are called to purity whether it interferes with your desires or not. When you live outside the God-ordained place of purity, you invite many sin complications: disease, pregnancy, affairs, etc. Those are sobering possible consequences. Were any of those consequences to enter your world, blaming God because He didn't take away your sex drive would not be an option. You would need to take full responsibility for those consequences yourself. The Bible is not an optional guidebook. We, His creation, are to obey it.

> *I know this sounds cranky, but you are called to purity whether it interferes with your desires or not.*

"Am I supposed to remain single the rest of my miserable life?" Misery is a choice. God in His sovereign design for your life does not will you to misery. He wills for you obedience to His Word and peace as you do what's best for your life.

In contrast to the preceding question, consider this desperate plea of a woman longing to be released from her marriage vow.

Dear Marilyn,

I thought I wanted to be married more than anything in life. I've been married for ten years. I'm bored, unfulfilled, and sure this marriage is not God's plan for my abundant life. I know God has a better plan for me. I missed it by marrying too soon. I can't believe a loving God would make me stick this out for the rest of my life.

—Trapped

I began this chapter by asking, "What do we do with feelings and longings that can't be satisfied and won't go away?" It seems wise to always examine our feelings and longings. In doing that we ask a few questions about the longings: are they reasonable, are they realistic, and are they morally acceptable? From there we decide if our thinking needs to be transformed.

Trapped, let's apply these questions to your longing to be free from your marriage. Is your longing reasonable? I would say it is reasonable. You're bored. Is your longing realistic? Probably not—few experiences in life measure up to our expectations. Is your longing morally acceptable? According to the world's standard, it is; according to God's standard, it is not.

It sounds as if the question we need to talk about is the "morally acceptable" one. Unless your husband is an adulterer, you do not have bibli-

> *Ask a few questions about the longings: are they reasonable, are they realistic, and are they morally acceptable?*

cal grounds for divorce. That being the case, let's consider your boredom. What aspect of your marriage is boring? Is your husband a bore? Does he know how to communicate his thoughts and feelings? Are his thoughts and feelings duller than dirt? In other words, figure out what's boring you. Also, do you have a pattern of being bored? Did you wander off in your mind while your English teacher explained the fascinating process of dia-gramming a sentence or the value of antecedents? If you hung on every word of all that, then you must be mar-ried to the world's dullest man! (Just a touch of humor.)

Actually, baby, my hunch is you have a pattern of feeling bored in other arenas of your life as well. While you're thinking that through, take the initiative to break the boredom cycle. What can you do to make your marriage more interesting? If the marriage is boring to you, chances are it's boring to your husband as well. Figure out a few fun things to do together. Ever try bowling? I took my grandchildren bowling a few months ago. I had not bowled in thirty years. As I lined up my ball with the pins and stepped adroitly down the lane to throw the ball, it would not let go of my thumb. The ball and I went hurtling down the lane together. Ian, my grandson, never recovered. He laughed helplessly all evening. My swollen thumb was worth the price of seeing Ian sprawled in a fit of laughter over my efforts to free my hand. Sometimes it doesn't take a lot to perk things up. Think about it, talk about it, and then do something about it.

And remember that God is sovereign. You didn't miss His plan. You may not like the plan, but God does what He does. I can fuss, but in the end it is His will that is accomplished. Ephesians 1:11 says, "All things happen just as he decided long ago" (NLT).

Does that mean we're all little robots with no will of our own? No, we are not little robots. I have yet to figure out how my will is figured into the sovereign equation of my life experience. But it is comforting to know my life is not a random shot propelled by either my bad choices or my good choices. God makes good of my bad choices as well. That's His promise.

> *It is comforting to know my life is not a random shot propelled by either my bad choices or my good choices. God makes good of my bad choices as well.*

The profound truth of the sometimes glibly quoted Romans 8:28 is a huge comfort to those of us who regret, worry, and blame ourselves for "missing the plan." I suggest to you, dear one, that God will bring good out of the marriage you're dying to get out of. I'd also suggest you may come to love the plan!

In the meantime, memorize Romans 8:28; it's definitely not boring! "And we know that God causes everything to work together for the good of those who love God and are called according to his purpose for them" (NLT).

We'll move off the subject of marriage with its

longings and onto the subject of parenting. It, too, has deep longings and many frustrations.

> Dear Marilyn,
>
> How should a mother relate to a child who is obviously living a sinful life—drugs, irresponsibility, sexual promiscuity, etc.? Shun, act as if everything is okay, give them money when they can't pay bills? By the way, where's God?
>
> —Heartbroken

Actually, this question and its answer are for anyone trying to deal with someone you love whose life is out of control from "sinful living." I hope the preceding discussion on God's sovereignty will be helpful to you as we consider some possible solutions for your child's behavior. We know that God never wills sin or tempts us to sin. We seem to manage that quite well on our own. God gets no blame for what we choose. We want to harbor in God's sovereignty and the sure knowledge that He will bring good out of life's "bad." In so doing, we will be made stronger and more aware of His provision. I believe it is possible to rest in Him, because we can trust in Him to be the God of everything.

Having reminded ourselves of this great harboring for our souls, let's talk a few practicalities. First, do not give your child money. Pay the food bill, the clothing bill, and any school bills yourself. Otherwise, whatever money your child receives will undoubtedly be used for drugs, etc. Even though that does not mean the money supply will dry up, it does mean you will not be contributing to it.

Do not shun your child, but by the same token, do not accept unacceptable behavior. Set boundaries. Don't change them. Decide what is not tolerable behavior, and communicate that with your child. Don't waver. Stay firm and be consistent. Join a 12-step group, which brings parents with the same kinds of kid issues together to support one another. And of course, do not pretend you don't know what's going on. You do know, so say so. In saying so, make it clear what kind of discipline you will use and when you will use it. And even as you maintain disciplinary standards, you need to communicate caring and love. When children are in a world of hurt, they usually show it through negative and often self-destructive behavior.

Now to my real concern: What is going on in the life of this child? Generally, this kind of behavior comes from acting out negative feelings rather than verbally expressing them. Have there been any major changes in your environment that may have thrown this kid out of balance? Are problems in your marriage producing fights and other disruptions? Has there been a move— new school, new neighborhood, loss of old friends? Might there be a school challenge you know nothing about—bullying or rejection? Are the grades slipping? Have you met with the teachers or the principal? Something's going on beyond the usual teen rebellion. Learn all you can.

Finally, you deserve to have a professional walk this path with you. Find a therapist who specializes in troubled teens. That professional will have local referrals in the event you need emergency care for your child. Please do not shrug off your own need for support.

Now that we've discussed the practical response, let's address your question, "By the way, where's God?" one more time. Though you may not feel Him or sense Him, God is right by your side. That's His promise to you and to your child. Remember, He is sovereignly orchestrating the details of your life in spite of appearances.

Since We're Chatting . . .

Nothing has been more liberating in my walk with the Lord than understanding and embracing the sovereignty of God. To say God is in charge frees me up *not* to be in charge. I don't know enough to be in charge. Though I will at times mumble about God's plan, I know His way is best for me. When I can't quite figure out what's going on, God can. That is reassuring. It is also reassuring that God invites my participation in what's going on.

For example, our first writer in this chapter, Miserable, is mad at God because she is not married. She believes she is doomed to a miserable life. Instead, she must participate in the transformation of her thinking. She can learn to accept the possibility that singleness is God's plan for her. She can also learn the many ways that singleness can lead to abundant living. Abundant living comes first from trusting and loving God, then loving others and serving their needs—an extension of God's love.

Mother Teresa clearly used her singleness in the service of others. She said that the biggest disease of her day was not leprosy or tuberculosis, but the feeling of being unwanted, uncared for, and deserted by everyone. Instead of bemoaning her single state, she worked to show the love of God to all those in need of health and care. I believe Mother Teresa lived the life God sovereignly designed for her.

I suggest that our bored young wife, Trapped, participate with God in ways to make her marriage rich instead of dull. It is reassuring to recognize that God will work His sovereign design in that relationship. She's not alone in working on their oneness; it is God's plan. He says, "The two shall become one." That's a position in which to rest.

Finally, there is nothing more heartbreaking than to see one's child derailed from all that has been taught about living as God intends. He wills purity and obedience. When that's not happening, how does God's sovereign design fit? We remember God does not author sin. God does not tempt us to sin. But when our willful and stubborn determinations lead us into "sinful living," God does not take His eyes off us, and neither does He stop caring. Jesus told the story of the prodigal son as an illustration of God the Father's relentless love for His wayward children. In the meantime, the parent watches, waits, and prays. Knowing God is in charge of that wayward child frees us to trust God's timing and accept His strength for our many weak moments.

Let's conclude these thoughts on the trustworthiness of God's sovereign love by reminding ourselves of these words from Psalms: "Everything God does is right—the trademark on all his works is love" (145:17 MSG). Where is God when we long for Him to change things? He's by our side, doing what

> *Knowing God is in charge of that wayward child frees us to trust God's timing and accept His strength for our many weak moments.*

He does for our well-being and for our growth in Him. He is working "all things according to the counsel of His will." I can rest in that; so can you.

SEVEN

MEET THE IN-LAWS

> This explains why a man leaves his father and
> mother and is joined to his wife.
>
> —*Genesis 2:24* NLT

There are at least a gazillion "mother-in-law" jokes in the world (which Rodney Dangerfield used to his personal advantage for years). The "problem" with in-laws is a popular topic for comics simply because most of us identify with at least some element of the humor, and we feel better when we can laugh about it. One of my favorite TV shows is *Everybody Loves Raymond*. The way this family functions is comforting. Raymond's mother doesn't care for his wife. The wife doesn't care much for her mother-in-law. And the father-in-law doesn't care much for anyone! Because they all live right next door to one another, they're always "underfoot," managing (or ignoring) one another's feelings. We come away saying, "At least my mother-in-law is not that bad!" We can smile to ourselves and move on.

One of my friends lived in dread as she anticipated her mother-in-law's annual visit. She would stay four or five months and then move on to visit her other son for four or five months. She was controlling, unpleasant, and negative. No matter what my friend cooked, the meals were criticized and left untouched on the plate. I suggested that might be a way to shorten her mother-in-law's life, but I suppose that was not good spiritual advice (even though it gave her a much needed giggle). The mother-in-law found fault with how the children were disciplined (or not disciplined), and even complained that the ghastly color scheme in the house gave her headaches. Always a spiritual encourager, I suggested the aspirin be hidden and the paint hues intensified. Tsk-tsk.

Sadly, my friend is not alone. Let's consider a few of the letters from other women struggling with the same issue.

Dear Marilyn,

My mother-in-law has been so mean to me through the years. I have been married to her son for almost twenty-three years. She has been a widow for all of those years. What advice can you give a daugh-

ter-in-law who wants to do the right thing and be
loving but has a hard time wanting to spend time
with or even desiring to talk with her mother-in-law
on occasion?

—Bullied

Here's a perfect example of how one reaps what one
sows. Your mother-in-law has been mean for twenty-
three years and will probably continue to be mean until
she dies. Her mean spirit has cost her a relationship with
you, her daughter-in-law. That's a tremendous loss to her
daily enrichment. In your situation, the challenge is to
do the right thing and be loving. Apparently, she has no
desire to rise to the challenge and return your kindness.
I respect and admire you all the more for your efforts.

Matthew 7:12 states the well-known golden rule—
"Do for others what you would like them to do for you.
This is a summary of all that is taught in the law and the
prophets" (NLT). You, dear one, are living according to
the command of the golden rule. You must be kind to
her, and your gestures to her must be loving. Does that
mean you must be a victim of her unkindness? Does
that mean that if she cuts you down with criticism and
barbed comments, you smile sweetly and say, "God
bless you"? I don't think so.

Is there any possibility you would feel brave enough
to tell her that her behavior and comments hurt you?

Might you risk telling her how much you would like to deepen your relationship with her, but you feel it is not possible without talking about what hurts you? I know this is risky and may stir things up even more. If she has been a widow for over twenty-three years, her patterns may be set in stone, and she may be unwilling to consider any other behavior.

I'm curious about your husband and his relationship with his mother. Is she mean to him? If so, she probably does have an unteachable spirit with no inclination to grow. If that's the case, I'd probably choose to keep my mouth shut. But that leaves us with the question, "How much do I take?" I don't think you are unreasonable to feel that spending time with her or talking to her is difficult. Some people are toxic. She sounds toxic. I suggest you check on her once every week. If she has further needs (doctor appointments, etc.), be as available as you are able. You are called to be kind, but

> *You are called to be kind, but you are not called to be a doormat.*

you are not called to be a doormat. Pull your husband (her son) into the responsibilities that come with her care. He needs to do his share with his mother.

Finally, pray for her. There is something healing to us personally as we pray for someone who is hurting us.

You are transferring your hurt to God, who in turn loves the one who hurt you. God needs to soften her heart. That's not your job. As you pray for her soul, heart, and spirit, your own spirit will soften as a result. It can be a win-win situation.

Our next question deals with the age-old challenge of how to respond to in-laws who are controlling.

> Dear Marilyn,
>
> I need some biblical support on how to deal with very controlling in-laws. My husband is currently deployed to Operation Iraqi Freedom, and my girls and I are trying to adjust to being by ourselves, but my in-laws keep dragging me down. I feel like they are trying to control my life. I love my in-laws very much, but how do I tell them to not be so controlling? I am thirty-one, and sometimes I feel like they think I am sixteen or younger. I do not want to say or do anything that I may regret. Please, if you have a biblical answer on how to deal with in-laws, I would love to have it.
>
> —All Grown Up

I can only imagine how difficult a time this must be for you. Having your husband deployed to Operation Iraqi Freedom is a huge stressor. You deal daily with the tension of his survival; the last thing you need is a fight for your own survival in his absence.

I am encouraged to read that you love your in-laws "very much." This gives you a foundation you can build upon in this time of tension for all of you.

They may not realize they are being controlling. They may not realize you feel they have no confidence in you. If your words are kindly communicated, you have the opportunity to deepen your relationship with them by telling them how you feel.

You could say something like:

"It means the world to me to have you here right now. I feel your love and support for me and for the girls at a time that is so hard for all of us. I fell in love with your son and thank God every day that you gave birth to him. I also thank God your son was given to me to be my husband and the father of my children.

"Sometimes I feel you may lack confidence in me to make good decisions for myself and for the girls while your son is in Iraq. Please know how much I value your wisdom and your advice. I want you to be involved in our daily lives. By the same token, I need to feel that my wisdom is also being acknowledged by you. If I'm doing something you question, you can of course talk to me. But in talking to me, remember I'm a capable thirty-one-year-old wife and mother who deeply cares about the well-being of her family.

"I have always appreciated the way you have loved me and welcomed me into your lives. Please know how deeply I love you and treasure our relationship. Thank you also for the confidence I feel that you will receive my words as you have always received my heart."

You asked for a biblical answer for dealing with your in-laws. We always want to live by the golden rule, but I'll also refer you to Isaiah 41:13, which cautions us not to live in fear: "For I, the LORD your God, will hold your right hand, saying to you, 'Fear not, I will help you.'"

All too often, we allow fear to dictate our behavior. If fear keeps you from having an authentic relationship with your in-laws, the result will be an aloofness that prevents understanding and caring between you not only in these present circumstances, but also in the future. There is a strained relationship between you right now. Don't let fear keep you separated from each other. As you speak the truth kindly, trust God to hold your hand and help you.

> *If fear keeps you from having an authentic relationship with your in-laws, the result will be an aloofness that prevents understanding and caring between you.*

Now, let's move to an in-law question that comes from the parents' perspective.

Dear Marilyn,

How do you deal with a daughter-in-law who acts nice around us but whom we know from what other people tell us is very mean-spirited to her children and her husband, our son. She professes to be a wonderful Christian person, but her example is very poor.

—Wary

I can imagine how you must worry about your grandchildren. What does "mean-spirited to her children" mean? It's one thing to be a short-tempered mom, and another if she takes her short temper and physically or emotionally uses it against the children. This may have the sound of "busybody" to it, but I would make every effort to learn what you can about how she treats the children. What exactly have others observed? Find out. Children are not able to protect themselves; someone has to ensure their safety. Your son ought to be able to take care of himself, but he certainly needs to take care of his children.

If your daughter-in-law is mean-spirited to your son as well, it sounds as if she's got a rotten case of "mad" going on. Not only does she have a case of "mad" going on, but she has a big case of "hypocrite" going on as well.

Your question, however, is not how to fix a "mad"

hypocrite, but how to deal with her yourself. Since all you have to go on is the report of others, I'd suggest you keep your mouth shut and your eyes and ears open. Sooner or later, something will blow her cover. I hope it will not be at the expense of her children's safety. In the meantime, pray and practice the golden rule. Isn't that hypocritical, you may ask? Not at all. The golden rule is carried out in service to God and His commands. Hypocrisy is carried out in service to the hypocrite and her need to look good. There is no godly element in hypocrisy.

Since We're Chatting . . .

As you would expect, God has a pattern for in-laws. Following those patterns could prevent a lot of in-law wallowing. To begin with, parents need to back off once their kids marry. The child does not lose obligations to parents when that child marries, but those obligations no longer come first. A husband's first obligation is to his wife and the wife's to her husband. Scripture does not say to cleave to parents after marriage. It says for the husband and wife to cleave to each other because they have become one.

My friend's mother was totally out of line with her four- and five-month visits to her son and daughter-in-law's house. Mama was cleaving. Son was allowing it. God's pattern was not being followed. Baby Boy needed to speak to Mama. Mama needed to get the first bus out of town. Before her next visit, she needs to be invited and then the length of the visit negotiated. She also needs to eat the food her daughter-in-law cooks, even if it necessitates filling her purse with Pepcid AC.

God's pattern for in-laws is mutual respect and kindness—the golden rule. There is a sweet story in Exodus 18, where Jethro is worried that his son-in-law Moses is working too hard. Jethro tells Moses there's no way he can keep up his current schedule without suffering in the process. Moses cuts back and is grateful for his father-in-law's loving counsel.

> *" Think of what the in-law scene would look like if the fruit of the Spirit splashed out all over everyone. "*

Galatians 5:22–23 describes the person whose interior world has been forever altered by the entrance of the Holy Spirit. "When the Holy Spirit controls our lives, he will produce this kind of fruit in us: love, joy, peace, patience, kindness, goodness, faithfulness, gentleness, and self-control" (NLT). Whew! Think of what the in-law scene would look like if the fruit of the Spirit splashed out all over everyone. These are virtues we all need in our hearts and lives. Even if our in-laws don't have them, we need to do our splashing anyway. God put a pattern in place, and it works. It might even contribute to soaring.

HE WANTS ME TO DO *WHAT*?

> *Marriage is a decision to serve the other, whether in bed or out.*
>
> —*1 Corinthians 7:4* MSG

Questions surrounding a wife's submission abound, especially when it comes to the bedroom. Consider this letter by a young woman who's wondering about the boundaries that she'd like to establish when it comes to intimate expressions.

Dear Marilyn,

    It seems to me that my friends and I are always wondering what God desires for us in our intimacy with our husbands. It seems apparent that men want more from women sexually than women want to give. What is a healthy boundary? I know we shouldn't say no all the time, or even too often. But what if husbands come up with new "ideas" that we don't feel comfortable with. What is a healthy boundary that protects the intimacy of the marital "bed" and also protects the feelings and emotions of both parties?

—Uncomfortable

And another letter . . .

Dear Marilyn,

I am thirty-five, and my peer group is always wondering about sex-related questions. Is oral sex biblically okay within marriage? Do we adhere to the Old Testament standards of sexual conduct and "clean and unclean" practices? All these types of questions are what we ladies end up discussing.

—Inquisitive

We don't have specific Bible verses that instruct us on the oral-sex issue. What we do have is the stated biblical intent of sexual expression: the two shall become one. That intent is not only for the body, but for the spirit and soul as well. The experience of oneness requires mutuality. The man loves the woman; the woman loves the man. Without mutuality, there is an imbalance that leads to the loss of divinely designed oneness.

First Corinthians 7:2–4 says the following:

> It's good for a man to have a wife, and for a woman to have a husband. Sexual drives are strong, but marriage is strong enough to contain them and provide for a balanced and fulfilling sexual life in a world of sexual disorder. The marriage bed must be a place of mutuality—the husband seeking to satisfy his wife, the wife seeking to satisfy her husband. Marriage is not a place to stand up for your rights. Marriage is a decision to serve the other, whether in bed or out. (MSG)

The straightforward language of *The Message* leaves little room for debate about the need for loving balance and mutuality in the husband-wife relationship. I especially love the energy of Paul's statement, "Marriage is not a place to stand up for your rights." Unfortunately, many

> *The experience of oneness requires mutuality. The man loves the woman; the woman loves the man.*

husbands feel they have biblical permission to stand up for their rights in regard to some sexual practices.

These practices may be totally unappealing to the

wife. In fact, they may be a huge turn-off for her. Using the words from the *New King James Version* for 1 Corinthians 7:4, "The wife does not have authority over her own body, but the husband does," can turn the marriage bed into a sexual battlefield. He claims biblical victory and domination; she retreats into guilty submission and, ultimately, emotional resentment. Oneness is lost. It is often at this point that the handy "headache" is used to avoid what has become an undesirable sexual experience.

So what do we do with the caveman "woman-come-here-your-body-is-mine-the-Bible-says-so" mentality? Once again we must remember that the original design for sex was instituted by God. It was not created to be used for dominance by either the male or the female. It was created as a means of tender and sensitive communication. It is meant to be an illustration of how Christ loves His church. Domination is utterly inappropriate and unscriptural. Jesus never forces His creatures to love Him against their will. His style is a persistent wooing that affirms the dignity of whoever is being wooed. It honors the other's response, whether it is positive or not.

Perhaps now we need to speak with greater specificity. The bottom line: "My husband wants oral sex; I hate it. He's mad, and I'm appalled." Now what? Don't forget: "Marriage is not a place to stand up for your rights. Marriage is a decision to serve the other, whether in bed or not." It is at this point that the spiritual head of the home, the man, is called upon to relinquish his right to be right. For the sake of loving his wife and nurturing her trust, the man yields his right to oral sex. He yields that right for the sake of oneness in his marriage. He does not "give in" to what he may consider a prudish point of view. He instead rises to a higher standard of loving. That loving is a commitment to oneness.

Stephen Arterburn's *Every Man's Marriage* has the finest discussion on male submission for the sake of oneness I have read. He suggests that to lose one aspect of the husband's preferred sexual expression does in reality bring great gain for the husband. The wife gains so much respect for his tender, non-demanding leadership that she doubles her commitment to give her body, mind, and spirit in the other areas of the marriage bed.

Paul writes on submission for the sake of oneness when he discusses whether one should eat meat. Paul felt that eating meat was not a spiritual issue, but he cautioned others to be sensitive to those who felt meat was "unclean." Let's refresh our minds on this topic by rereading Romans 14:14–18. The passage speaks to our need for an attitude of graciousness even though we may not agree with the point of view held by others. The implications of this passage carry over to our sensitive topic of what is appropriate for the marriage bed.

I know and am perfectly sure on the authority of the Lord Jesus that no food, in and of itself, is wrong to eat. But if someone believes it is wrong, then for that person it is wrong. And if another Christian is distressed by what you eat, you are not acting in love if you eat it. Don't let your eating ruin someone for whom Christ died. Then you will not be condemned for doing something you know is all right.

For the Kingdom of God is not a matter of what we eat or drink, but of living a life of goodness and peace and joy in the Holy Spirit. If you serve Christ with this attitude, you will please God. (NLT)

What's the teaching here? What is okay for you may not be okay for someone else. With love and caring, you do not insist on your own belief system. Instead, for the sake of Christian oneness, you yield your preference, which then produces "goodness and peace and joy in the Holy Spirit." We are assured that this attitude pleases God.

Let's cap this discussion off with the reminder we receive from Romans 15:1–3.

We may know that these things make no difference, but we cannot just go ahead and do them to please ourselves. We must be considerate of the doubts and fears of those who think these things are wrong. We should please others. If we do what helps them, we will build them up in the Lord. For even Christ didn't please himself. (NLT)

The husband is called to honor the wife's reluctance or refusal to engage in oral sex. Why? "We cannot just go ahead and . . . please ourselves. We must be considerate of the doubts and fears of those who think these things are wrong. We should please others." The scriptural call to the husband is to help build the wife's relationship with the Lord through his own godly example of caring and sensitive love.

Once again, Scripture states over and over again the importance of living out of love for all those with whom we are in relationship. It's hard to fight and love at the same time. The best action is to give up fighting for our rights and instead snuggle into each others' arms, knowing God is pleased with

> *The scriptural call to the husband is to help build the wife's relationship with the Lord through his own godly example of caring and sensitive love.*

our mutual submission. When we experience God's pleasure, we also experience His peace. What a great reward for what had formerly been a climate of striving and marital unrest.

Since We're Chatting . . .

A couple I was counseling was struggling with under-standing one of the many consequences of child-hood sexual abuse: flashbacks. The wife had been regularly forced to give and receive oral sex from her teenage brother. It started when she was ten; the brother was fourteen. The abuse continued until the brother left for college when he was seventeen.

At first the wife had few specific memories of the abuse, but over a period of time the counseling and flash-backs encouraged the memories to surface. For her, the knowledge resulted in a total aversion to anything sexual, including kissing. Prior to the flashbacks, the wife had been sexually responsive. Her sudden revulsion was confusing to them both.

The husband was brokenhearted over the knowl-edge of his wife's abuse. His compassion and tenderness were a source of great encouragement and healing as her memories gradually emerged from that soul cellar where they'd been buried. He asked her permission to continue attending the counseling sessions. He wanted desperately to understand his wife's pain but did not want to inter-fere if his presence would be a problem. She gratefully welcomed him.

At one point, she asked him if he would continue to

love her and wait for her until she was no longer afraid of anything physical. She asked him if he would hold her but not kiss her or touch her. She also asked him if he would promise to never, ever expect oral sex. The act filled her with terror, and she knew she would never be able to do it again. He tenderly promised to wait forever if it was necessary; he didn't want to do anything that would fill her with terror.

I was continually stunned by this husband's almost "too good to be true" tenderness for his wife. In that session I've just described, I burst out with, "You love your wife like Jesus does." He looked a little startled. He told me then that his father was a pastor whose harsh treatment of his wife left enormous scars on the entire family. His father preached "submission and domination" of all women. That, according to him, was the Bible's teaching. My client said, "I determined at a young age that I would love my future wife in all the ways my father never loved my mother. And," he continued, "I also determined I wanted nothing to do with the god of my father."

The god of his father is in no way the God we know from reading Scripture. The God we read about in the Bible is visible to us in the person of Jesus. Jesus modeled compassion and caring for all women. It would never be in the character of God to subject women to a position of worthlessness or servitude. The fact that God would institute a loving "head" for the wife as insurance that she would always be provided for, nurtured, and honored is one of the most gracious gifts women can receive.

The fact that God's gift is so abused and misunderstood is a great triumph for the enemy. The goal of the enemy is to distort and pervert the truth. His goal is to enslave all who will listen. God's goal is to set us free, and it was accomplished on the cross. To borrow the phrase from T. D. Jakes, "Woman, thou art loosed."

The man who submits to these biblical truths and loves his "loosed" woman in the way Jesus does is the man no woman can resist. The man who refuses to stand up for his rights and does not insist on his own preferred bedroom practices is the man demonstrating godly love.

In case you're curious about the outcome of the couple's therapy, for two years, they never had any sexual contact at all. Gradually, she became comfortable with some kissing. They made a deal that she would signal what she felt comfortable with as they worked through the emotional residue of her abuse. These traumas to the soul are never quick work, but this couple diligently determined to come together again—mind, body, and soul—no matter how long it took.

When we had our final session, I knew beyond a shadow of a doubt that emotional healing had occurred and new thinking was taking over. There was much scarring as a result of her abuse. But a scar does not continue to bleed like a wound does. I watched these two courageous people walk out of my office no longer bleeding. It was a "Thank you, Jesus" moment.

NINE

LOOKING FOR LOOPHOLES

> *"Is it lawful for a man to divorce his wife for just any reason?"*
>
> —*Matthew 19:3*

J ust in case you are hoping for a divorce loophole somewhere in Scripture, remind yourself of Jesus' words found in Matthew 19:3–6:

The Pharisees came to Him, testing Him, and saying to Him, "Is it lawful for a man to divorce his wife for just any reason?" And He answered and said to them, "Have you not read that He who made them at the beginning 'made them male and female,' and said, 'For this reason a man shall leave his father and mother and be joined to his wife, and the two shall become one flesh'? So then, they are no longer two but one flesh. Therefore what God has joined together, let not man separate."

The reason the Pharisees kept pressing the divorce issue was based on their desire to trap Jesus into a statement that would discredit Him. So they said:

"Why then did Moses command to give a certificate of divorce, and to put her away?" He said to them, "Moses, because of the hardness of your hearts, permitted you to divorce your wives, but from the beginning it was not so. And I say to you, whoever divorces his wife, except for sexual immorality, and marries another, commits adultery; and whoever marries her who is divorced commits adultery." (Matt. 19:7–9)

It is obvious what Jesus thinks of divorce. Divorce destroys marriage—a relationship so holy, so sacred that the loyalties of the marriage relationship come even before that of children and their parents. The whole teaching of the Bible relative to marriage is that it is a holy relationship uniting one man and one woman until they are separated by death. The Bible gives only two situations in which divorce is allowable. Christ discusses sexual immorality in Matthew 19:9, and Paul discusses desertion in 1 Corinthians 7:15 (a passage we will revisit in chapter 10). So there you have it. I've saved you the time of looking for any other scriptural loopholes for divorce. Except for sexual immorality and desertion, there's no wiggle room. There's no other loophole. Marriage is designed above all else to be a holy relationship. Let no one mess with it.

"But hey, wait a minute, Marilyn. What about 2 Corinthians 6:14? I am trapped in a marriage with a non-Christian. Isn't that a loophole?" Let's look at that passage: "Do not be unequally yoked together with unbelievers. For what fellowship has righteousness with lawlessness? And what communion has light with darkness?"

According to the definitive teaching Jesus gave in Matthew, even the dark-versus-light issue is not a loophole. That unequally yoked relationship undoubtedly brings many challenges. God is not indifferent to those challenges. He invites you to call upon Him in the time of trouble. He promises to never leave you or forsake you, but He does not back down on the sanctity of the institution of marriage. The bottom line: God has ordained marriage. It is His idea; it is His plan.

The following letter describes the pain of being unequally yoked in marriage:

Dear Marilyn,

I knew my fiancé was not a Christian before I married him, but I was sure he would change. Before we married he wanted to please me in everything. He always said, "Maybe one day your beliefs will make sense to me." We have been married for ten years. We have two adorable boys—eight and six years old. My husband used to be tolerant of my Bible study and church attendance. Now, he is hostile toward anything about my faith. He encourages our two boys to stay home with him on Sunday morning instead of going to Sunday school. He tells them church and Sunday school are for sissies, not men. It's breaking my heart to see what my husband's influence is having on the boys. I want desperately to get away from his influence. In fact, I want desperately to get away from him as well. He is selfish, unkind, and totally indifferent to me in everything. It makes no sense that I have to stay in this marriage.

—Unequally Yoked

It makes perfect sense that you want desperately to be released from your wedding vow of "'til death do us part." You undoubtedly feel that you are in a "death walk" now as you battle the darkness of your husband's influence and point of view. I am so sorry. So is God. Scripture says God's intent for marriage is spiritual oneness for the body, soul, and spirit. That "God goal" was not altered when the first creation chose to disobey, but the fall did make that goal more difficult to achieve. The sin nature is in continual battle against the God goal. That's why we need Spirit power to live as God wills us to live. Living according to God's original plan is not impossible. Difficult, but not impossible.

You, dear one, have chosen a difficult path. Knowing your husband was not a believer but marrying him anyway was not a wise choice. However, you are on a path where the light of God never fails to shine. You do not live in darkness as long as Jesus, the Light of the World, lives and radiates within you. You made a mistake. We all make mistakes. That's why Scripture compares us to sheep. Sheep are not the brightest bulbs in the pasture. They need a loving, vigi-

> *You are on a path where the light of God never fails to shine.*

lant shepherd who is always watching out for the needs of his flock. Why must he constantly keep an eye on the sheep? Isaiah 53:6 gives us the answer: "All of us have strayed away like sheep. We have left God's paths to follow our own" (NLT). God is our tireless Shepherd and our inextinguishable Light. Though we all make sheep like mistakes, God continues to light our illchosen path and never stops loving us. Let's be reminded again of that love: "I have loved you, my people, with an everlasting love. With unfailing love I have drawn you to myself" (Jer. 31:3 NLT). This love is ours whether we act like sheep or not.

So now, let's talk about the specifics of your situation: a spiritually and emotionally indifferent husband and a spiritually negative influence on your boys. Can you walk off and leave him? Sweet baby, there's no biblical wiggle room out of your marriage. But hear God's promise to you as you stay right where you are. It's found in Isaiah 58:10–11. (*Love* that book of Isaiah!)

"Then your light will rise in darkness,
And your gloom will become like midday.
And the LORD will continually guide you,
And satisfy your desire in scorched places.
And give strength to your bones;
And you will be like a watered garden,
And like a spring of water whose waters do not fail." (NASB)

Let's talk about God transforming you into a new person by changing the way you think. At this point, you may think the biblical "no wiggle room" is like a jail sentence. You're stuck behind the bars of a choice you now regret. But God in His sovereign plan for your life wills that "light will rise in darkness" and that your "gloom will become like midday." So think thoughts of light. Let me suggest the following "light thoughts":

1. This marital darkness will become light. I need not think thoughts of despair. I will think thoughts that assure me of God's love for me no matter what my choices have been.

2. I will not despair for my children. I will entrust them to God's sovereign care, reminding myself that those little boys belong to God. I will live out God's love for them as I teach them about Jesus the Savior, God the Creator, and the love the divine Father feels for them. I will trust this light message will penetrate their little souls in spite of the competing darkness they hear about and witness from their daddy.

3. I choose to think and believe that God will "continually guide" me. I am not out there alone, wandering lost upon the mountains of my choice.

4. I choose to believe and think that He intends to "give strength to my bones." When I falter and feel weak, I will know He strengthens me.

5. I choose to believe and therefore think my life will not be a "scorched place" but a "watered garden." That's God's promise to me.

6. With God's enablement, I choose to think kind thoughts about my husband. I will be to him an example of God's love. I will not return the arrows of reproach he may sling at me. I choose to live by the golden rule. I will treat him the way I want to be treated.

I wish you well, sweetheart. Take yet another Isaiah promise with you as you begin this new leg of your journey: "He will give beauty for ashes, joy instead of mourning, praise instead of despair" (61:3 NLT).

Does it not seem reasonable the following writer should have a "loophole"?

Dear Marilyn,

My husband and I have been married for twenty-six years. We have two daughters who are now married. For weeks at a time, my husband refuses to speak to me or even acknowledge my presence. He acts like he's always mad at me.

I've tried to talk to him to find out what's wrong. He always says, "You're what's wrong." I don't know what I've done that is so wrong. I guess it's that I'm still breathing and taking up space in the house. He refuses counseling. I went for two years, and it helped me with self-esteem. But I'm so lonely and long to be loved. I think he hates me.

I am a Christian, and he says he is too. We go to church together, but he rarely speaks to anyone there. He never talks about his faith. I'm not sure he has any. My daughters have begged me for years to leave him. They hate what it's doing to my health and what it's always done to my emotions. As far as I know he's never slept with anyone. I wish he had so I could be free. By the way, we have separate bedrooms.

—Locked Out

Well, baby, he sounds like a nightmare. It would be better if he *were* a nightmare, because at least then you could wake up. Just out of curiosity, what was his mother like? What was his father like? Were either of them smoldering volcanoes waiting to erupt? Knowing that information will not answer the question of whether you should or should not walk out of the relationship, but it might help you understand that his "manner" is not about you. My guess is that he is carrying on the family tradition of "sourpussness" and vindictive blaming for all that's wrong with the world. I am so sorry. You do not deserve that toxic environment, nor do you deserve to live in a loveless, nonnurturing marriage. Your husband obviously does not have a clue how to love you as Christ loves His church.

That being the case, I would like to refer you to the verse that says, "If you're married to an angry, vindictive man, fold up thy tent and leave forthwith." The problem with that verse is that it has yet to be written. There are many times I would like to toss in a few verses of Scripture that, it seems to me, should have been written but weren't.

Biblically speaking, you do not have grounds for

divorce. You could possibly justify separation—leave him and begin a life free of his toxicity. But in essence, you are already separated. He tries to pretend you do not exist. Apparently, he does not enter your bedroom, so you have left each other already. The advantage to you in a physical separation would be that the fumes from his anger would not constantly be in your nostrils. I would not suggest separation if he were teachable or sensitive to the teachings of Scripture. He has a biblical mandate to love his wife as Jesus loves His church. He has failed miserably. Under the circumstances, even though divorce is not an option, perhaps separation is. It seems unlikely, but perhaps a move will jar him into reconsidering his behavior as a husband.

So how about this little spitfire?

Dear Marilyn,

I want a divorce! My husband has had two affairs (that I know of) during our ten-year relationship, and I've just learned he's "at it again." I am sick of him, sick of pretending to the kids that "Daddy has to work late again," and sick of the church! Our pastor counseled us last year and basically told me I had to forgive my husband and give him another chance. Word of our marital problems leaked out to a few church people (primarily the deacon board), and they sided with the pastor that I needed to forgive and forget as God does. Their stand was that God does not run out of forgiveness, and neither should I. I'm here to tell you I am totally out of forgiveness, totally out of patience, and totally out of love! I hate to ask, but what do you say?

—Fed Up

I'm with you! I think you should search for a lawyer with barracuda tendencies. I also think you should search for a new church. You are entitled to receive the love of Jesus from the church, not a lack of empathy or the decision that repeated infidelities must be received with repeated bushels of forgiveness. Jesus told the woman caught in adultery to "go and sin no more." He didn't tell her to hang out with people who overlooked her transgressions and then said, "Oh well."

To begin with, you have scriptural grounds for divorce. Your husband's multiple infidelities push him into the adulterer lineup; there is no question he is qualified to wear the label. What is especially troubling about his behavior is that he appears to have had no remorse. When he's inspired again, he repeats his sin again.

I do not advocate divorce lightly. If true repentance occurs and sincere efforts are made to heal the splinters flying off the marriage structure, I'm in favor of putting the pieces back together again. Marriage is the toughest relationship there is to maintain. It requires tenacity and determination to talk through and work out differences. But breaking the sexual trust bond in marriage is a major violation of the sanctity of that marriage. Separating, splitting, or diminishing in value what God has put together is a serious offense, not to be taken with a casual tsk-tsk. We know God says in Malachi 2:16 that He hates divorce. He also hates the sin that permits divorce.

So, little spitfire, let's get a few practical concerns taken care of. I suggest you get a barracuda lawyer, because it is crucial that you and your children are financially supported. I've seen too many women cave in with a lawyer who does not fairly and aggressively represent them. Your attitude is not to be vindictive ("I'll take you for everything you've got, buddy"), but responsible ("I'm making sure our children are not going to suffer financially"). That's fair. Scout around for a lawyer whose reputation is that of a balanced but strong person whom you can trust to defend your needs effectively.

Equally crucial to your financial security is the security of your children. I think divorce is harder for children that many parents fully realize. Many children take on the blame for the divorce. They think if they had just been better kids, gotten better grades, or understood math, maybe Mom and Dad would still be together. While their reasoning may be illogical, they still suffer enormous personal guilt. Although the children cannot always internalize the words "It is not your fault," you need to lovingly and repeatedly give them that verbal message.

And now, baby, we need to talk about your anger. You have every human reason to be spittin' mad. You've been horrifically betrayed by your husband. Your church has not come alongside you and offered non-judgmental, unconditional love. They have instead shot you with some Bible bullets meant to shame you into submission. That is not the behavior of a church meant to be a haven for the hurting. It is not the behavior of Jesus, who is head of the church. You want to keep your eyes on the Shepherd and not the sheep. Remember, sheep are dull bulbs. But for reasons I'll never understand, Jesus loves those dull bulbs and volunteered to die for them. Why? So they would not have to. That's amazing love. That's also amazing forgiveness. Jesus is our model for how to love and how to forgive. You will, with God's enablement, want to forgive your husband. You will want to forgive because Jesus tells us to. You also will want to forgive because a lack of forgiveness will turn you into an angry, bitter mom

> *He truly may be a candidate for regeneration and change. If indeed that is God's sovereign design for you both, keep an eye out for God's flawless creativity.*

who will talk mean about the children's daddy. That will do great harm to the children. You may choke on the words, but you always need to speak positively about him to them. He may not deserve it, but your children do.

And finally, sweet baby, once you've gotten all the legal stuff in place, slow your pace. There's the off chance this two-timin' husband of yours may see his sin and fully repent. He truly may be a candidate for regeneration and change. If indeed that is God's sovereign design for you both, keep an eye out for God's flawless creativity. He's been known to orchestrate some pretty big events in some very dramatic ways. Prepare to be amazed . . . just in case.

Since We're Chatting . . .

Can you believe one out of every two marriages ends in divorce? Can you believe those divorces occur within the first ten years of marriage? Can you believe these statistics are the same for Christians as for those in the secular world? What's going on in our heads, in our hearts, in our spiritual beings? These are sobering statistics that scream out "something is very wrong" with our concept of marriage.

As we have reminded ourselves from Scripture, marriage is God's crown jewel. He designed it for His people that we might experience human oneness. He designed sexual expression to literally illustrate that oneness as two come together. God feels so strongly about marriage, He makes it nearly impossible to sever the bond of marriage and is deeply grieved when we do. Since marriage is a very big deal to God, why isn't it a big deal to us?

For one thing, I wonder how many of us truly understand God's feeling about marriage. Unless there is a specific reason to study God's unalterable view of marriage, most of us may move on to other topics in Scripture, forgetting one of the most crucial messages God has for each of us. "A man shall leave his father and mother and be joined to his wife, and they shall become one flesh" (Gen. 2:24). And of course there is the ominous addendum added to that Scripture: "What God has joined together, let not man [or woman] separate" (Mark 10:9).

In addition to being biblically illiterate about God's view of marriage, I wonder if there is a mind-set in many persons that says, "If this doesn't work, I'll simply get out of it." We are a society prone to disposing of that which we no longer find useful. "Trade it in for a better one," we say, and so we generally do. Now, of course, there is great convenience with our disposables; they rid our homes of clutter and provide much-needed time to purchase more disposables. However, 50 percent of our population appears to believe marriage is disposable. If it no longer pleases us, if it ceases to meet our needs, and if what we thought we were getting is in fact not what we got, trade it in. "Surely God does not mean for us to be miserable," we say. And then we add, "Didn't Jesus promise abundant life? This marriage totally lacks abundant-life potential." So what does one do? Trade it in for a new and hopefully better one next time around. While popular, this approach is the opposite of God's intent for marriage, a lifetime commitment.

> *The unfortunate truth about feelings is that they have no brains and they're prone to change.*

I believe one of the ways we might bring the divorce rate down is to recognize the imperative value of premarital counsel. Many couples are of the opinion that their feelings for each other will enable them to weather any marital storm. The unfortunate truth about feelings is that they have no brains and they're prone to change. I'm not discounting the value of feelings, but they do not provide a firm foundation. The most important element for the long-term health of the wedding vow is the degree to which the couple is committed to those vows no matter what the future holds. Commitment is necessary for those times when the spouse proves moody, forgetful, focused on sports, and prone to leaving clothing on the floor. Commitment is necessary when unexpected financial needs strain the marriage. When feelings change, commitment cannot change.

Reality-based, Bible-based premarital counsel can shift the focus of a relationship from the romantic to the practical. Valuable insights come as a man and woman hash through their communication patterns. Does one talk and the other withdraw as soon as he or she senses danger? How were differences dealt with by their parents? There's a strong possibility that those patterns will be hauled into the marriage. Did they work? If not, how should they be changed? A couple usually needs help in learning conflict-resolution skills. That there will be conflict is a given. However, that conflict does not have to drive a wedge between the two if they learn how to maintain each other's dignity and integrity. To do that, they need to know how to talk to each other.

My hope is that couples will recognize the need for delving into their deeper selves. The richness they discover in each other will be worth the time and effort.

There are, of course, many other topics for premarital counseling that can help avert painful separation. It is imperative to be well educated on the human issues as well as the spiritual issues as a couple embarks upon that great sea of matrimony. My hope is that couples will recognize the need for delving into their deeper selves. The richness they discover in each other will be worth the time and effort. And I believe that effort will bring the divorce rate down. It will also lessen the inclination to wallow.

INTERMISSION

Medical research is wonderfully clear about the benefits of laughter for the body. We know laughter relaxes the skeletal frame, lowers blood pressure, releases those little endorphin painkillers, and expands the blood vessels. What is new in medical research is the benefit of laughter for that often ignored but vitally important organ—the liver. Apparently, laughter is the one human activity that exercises the liver. I never knew the liver was in need of exercise, but just knowing laughter does for my liver what laughter does for my blood pressure causes me to dash about for daily humor with the well-being of my liver in mind.

No one has helped exercise my liver more than my friend Luci. When the pain of life bears down, the questions are overwhelming, and the answers come more slowly, laughter is the best medicine.

Our Women of Faith conferences are known for the

many extraordinary musical artists who perform with us. We've had fabulous experiences with artists like Stephen Curtis Chapman, Amy Grant, CeCe Winans, Kristen Chenowith, Sandi Patty, Nicole Nordeman, and many others who include Women of Faith in their busy performance schedules. One of my favorite groups is Avalon. They not only do "knock-ya-down-drag-you-around" fantastic musical presentations, but they're warm, fun, and compelling human beings who love Jesus.

During one of their weekends with us, we were sitting in the green room laughing and sharing crazy stories. Many of my most memorable moments are times Luci and I have managed to get one another in a little trouble. When that happens, one of us ends up buying the other one's dinner. That day, the story-telling backstage prompted Jody McBrayer, one of the Avalon soloists, to say to me as we were walking to our seats "Marilyn, aren't you up to speak next?"

"Yeah."

"Well, I have a great idea, but I'm not going to tell you what it is until we walk out of here and head for the stage." Of course I was intrigued.

So, as we exited the green room, Jody fell into step with me and said, "I'll give you fifty bucks if you can somehow work the word *ringworm* into your speech." I hooted.

"Are you kidding, Jody—*ringworm*?"

"Yup! It's worth fifty bucks to me to see if you can

somehow weave that word into whatever you say this afternoon. But the deal is, you have to make it seem to fit." I was hooked.

"Okay, Jody. But I'll have to have more than fifty bucks. I'll need one hundred. I mean, really, *ringworm* is worth a hundred."

He thought for a second and said, "Okay, but remember, *ringworm* has to make sense. You can't just shout the word out of the blue."

"You've got a deal, Jody!"

I then took my seat on the porch. With only a few moments for deep-think, I leaned over to Luci and whispered, "Do you mind if I say you have ringworm?"

"What . . . ?"

"Do you mind if I say that you have ringworm?"

She snorted back, "I don't have ringworm . . . never have had ringworm, you birdbrain . . . what are you talking about?"

"Jody will pay me a hundred bucks if I can work the word *ringworm* into my speech. Can I say you have it? I'll take you to lunch with the victory money." Her eyes brightened, the deal was made, and I went onstage.

Each week toward the end of my speech, I describe a time Luci recently popped by my house with Starbucks. In that time, we caught up on stuff and exercised our livers. As she was exiting my driveway, for some reason she was not backing out in a straight line but was slowly veering into my newly planted petunias. It was at this point in my speech that I decided to change the story line and throw in the word *ringworm*. So I told the audience I hated to correct Luci as she backed into my petunias, because she has periodic outbreaks of ringworm. I worried that maybe her medication was too strong this time. I explained that one of the little-known side effects of ringworm medication is an overwhelming desire to be enveloped by petunias. So actually, I could not really fault her for veering into my petunias—it was a drug-induced response. The audience registered a combination of sympathy, confusion, and disbelief. Luci was beaming in anticipation of a free lunch and seemingly not the slightest bit concerned about her false skin condition or that I had made it a matter of public knowledge.

I had not had time to warn the porch pals, so they were hooting with this unexpected touch of craziness. Luci jumped to her feet as Jody dashed over to hug her. They did a little dance while I explained to the audience that Luci did not really have ringworm. I told them I had just earned a hundred bucks from Jody, who bet me I could not work the word *ringworm* into my speech. Actually, I was the one who felt like doing a victory dance. Once all that was made clear, the audience joined in with enthusiastic cheering and clapping.

So there you have it, dear ones: a little exercise for our livers. Thanks, Jody, from all of us!

TEN

I WANT TO
START OVER

> *Therefore, if anyone is in Christ, he is a new creation; old things have passed away; behold, all things have become new.*
>
> *—2 Corinthians 5:17*

Now that all organs are tuned up, let's jump into the very difficult topic of what Scripture says about remarriage after divorce. There is a lot of confusion and pain regarding this subject, as you well know.

Since Scripture is so clear on God's feeling about divorce, what, if any, are the options for one who is the innocent object of unfaithfulness? What does the innocent one do? Can she remarry? Does one then get the label "adulterer" for having remarried, even though it was the former spouse who was unfaithful? Dare we say it seems a bit cranky of God to make the innocent suffer for someone else's behavior? Surely the innocent have a right to experience marital harmony and oneness with a new partner—don't they?

Let's talk about the following letter and consider possible biblical options for its writer.

Dear Marilyn,

My daughter has been married for twenty-three years and has two children. Her husband has been unfaithful five times during that time. She doesn't believe in divorce, and if she were to get one, she would not want to spend the rest of her life alone. (I have been a widow for thirty-two years but have been relatively happy.) She says she doesn't want to commit adultery if she remarries.

—Looking for Hope

Let's reread Jesus's statement in Matthew 19: "Whoever divorces his wife, except for sexual immorality, and marries another, commits adultery" (v. 9). God hates divorce, and He hates immorality, but immorality frees the innocent spouse from the label of adulterer even if she remarries. Did you hear that? God does provide an option for the innocent spouse. He does give permission for that innocent one to experience harmony, unity, and oneness in a remarriage experience.

Dear writer, in answer, let me address your daughter directly. Sweet baby, God gives you permission to leave your husband—who has committed adultery five times—and marry someone else. Your husband appears to be stubbornly resistant to change. He appears to care nothing for your feelings and the humiliation he causes you. He is morally guilty. Would you like to leave? Knowing God made provision for you to leave an unfaithful husband, do you want to be free?

Somehow, I have a sense you have become accustomed to your marriage and your husband's infidelities. Perhaps there are other rewards for you in the marriage that you don't want to give up. They may be spiritual, financial, social, or even emotional influences that cause you to stay put. That is a choice you make. But I would hate for you to stay because you think you would not be allowed to biblically remarry. God makes that allowance for you.

Let's consider now yet another provision God makes for the innocent spouse.

Dear Marilyn,

My husband and I were married for six years. One morning he announced he did not love me and thought he probably never had. He moved out that day, saying he hoped someone would come along and love me like I deserved. I later received divorce papers citing "irreconcilable differences." We had no children.

Now, four years later, I have fallen in love with a wonderful Christian man who wants to marry me. I'm struggling with this because, as far as I know, my husband was not unfaithful to me sexually. My understanding of the Bible is that I can't remarry or I would be an adulterer. Does the Bible say anything about people like me? If it does, I sure can't find it. The only thing I read is that God hates divorce and remarriage is not an option.

—Deserted

Yes, the Bible does say something about people like you, and it's good news for you. Let me first say, however, that I am deeply indebted to the scholarship of Chuck Swindoll, who ably tackles this topic of remarriage in his book *Getting Through the Tough Stuff*. It was his study that pointed me to 1 Corinthians 7 and its teaching regarding desertion. This is a chapter we all need to read and study carefully, especially those whose marriages are threatened.

As it relates to marital desertion, 1 Corinthians 7:15 states: "But if the unbeliever departs, let him depart; a brother or a sister is not under bondage in such cases. But God has called us to peace." Perhaps you, like me, would benefit from some studied commentary on this verse. Chuck quotes R. C. H. Lenski in his book *The Interpretation of St. Paul's First and Second Epistles to the Corinthians*. Lenski writes:

From that day onward, the fetters of the marriage tie have been broken and remain so, now and indefinitely. The deserting spouse broke them. No law binds the unbelieving spouse . . . .

It goes without saying that a believing spouse will by Christian kindness and persuasion do all that can be done to prevent rupture. But when these fail, Paul's verdict is: "Thou are free!"

Desertion is exactly like adultery in its effect. Both disrupt the marriage tie . . . The essence of marriage is union. When this is disrupted, the union which God intended to be a permanent one is destroyed; sinfully destroyed. There is only this difference in the case of adultery, the innocent spouse may forgive and continue the marriage, or may accept the dire result, the sundering of the marriage. In the case of desertion the former is not possible; the deserted spouse can no longer continue a marriage for none exists.

Many deserted women live under the bondage of their desertion and their fear that remarriage is not an option. According to Dr. Lenski's interpretation of 1 Corinthians 7:15, the deserted wife is under no obligation to stay in a marriage that no longer exists.

The word *bondage* here is specifically understood to

mean "to be bonded." It is not referring to the emotional feeling of bondage, but to the actual bond of matrimony. When the bond is broken, discarded, or no longer acknowledged, the marriage no longer binds.

What about remarriage for the writer of the following letter?

Dear Marilyn,

I foolishly chose to leave home at age seventeen to marry a man ten years older than me. I thought he was exciting. I thought he would be the first man to really love me. He turned out to be a man who loved his alcohol and cocaine more than he ever loved me. He physically abused me and our two boys. He had multiple sexual flings. So did I. During one of his insane anger fits, I took the boys and ran away to a women's shelter. I learned about God there. I learned that He wants to be my Father. It all seemed too good to be true. I'm learning that it really is true. I want to get my life together again, remarry, and give my boys a Christian home now. I was raised in a Christian home, but my father had a violent temper. The counselor at the shelter says I can't remarry because my husband is still alive. I don't have a man in my life, but what if I find a Christian man and want to marry him?

—Fresh Start

The comfort for you is found in 2 Corinthians 5:17: "Therefore, if anyone is in Christ, he is a new creation; old things have passed away; behold, all things have become new." In your old self, you had sexual flings. In your old self, you showed poor judgment in leaving home as a minor and marrying a drug-using alcoholic. But though you were raised in what you say was a Christian home, you saw little if any evidence of what that meant. Now, in your new self, you are learning that God is your Father. You are learning that the best way to live is to have a Christian home for you and your boys. Your new self wants to marry a Christian. I see and hear that a change has occurred in your life. You are turning from sin. You are leaving darkness for light. Ephesians 4 describes what is happening to you:

> Everything—and I do mean everything connected with that old way of life has to go. It's rotten through and through. Get rid of it! And then take on an entirely new way of life—a God-fashioned life, a life renewed from the inside and working itself into your conduct as God accurately reproduces his character in you. (vv. 22–24 MSG)

Since you are a new person, you are getting a new start. Your new start began with your conversion to Jesus, who died on the cross for all sin. As a result, your sins are forgotten by God—what an amazing truth. In fact, He says in Jeremiah 31:34, "I will forgive their wickedness and will never again remember their sins" (NLT). You truly start with a clean slate the moment you confess your sin and receive Jesus as your Savior.

Now, in your new person, you can look for a husband who is also walking in newness of life. You will want to be very aware that old patterns can creep back into your new life. Be conscious of the decisions you make. Be sure those decisions are guided by the Spirit of God who lives within you. My suggestion to you, dear writer, is don't hurry the new-husband search. You have a lot of personal healing to do, and so do your boys. That comes first. Though I believe you have scriptural grounds for remarriage, you have psychological and emotional issues that need immediate prayerful and professional attention. Marriage can wait. Your internal healing cannot.

Since We're Chatting . . .

The contemplation of remarriage is not to be taken lightly. God is exceedingly specific about what He wants for us, His children. Of course, we make poor choices and sometimes blatantly disobey God's commands. When disobedience to God's Word occurs in the life of the believer, there are always consequences. The sin of disobedience needs to be confessed. God is faithful to forgive that sin, but our destructive decisions leave consequences. There is always a negative payoff for sin. That payoff may come in the shape of personal guilt, remorse, and shame. It may be shaped in the knowledge that innocent people's lives have been forever altered because of our choices. It may come in the form of children who feel betrayed and confused. We need to recognize that when we choose to step away from the divine order, we are not able to experience God's original best for us.

What is God's original best? One marriage between two people committed to spiritual unity. That spiritual unity produces mutual caring and commitment for each other's human needs as well as spiritual needs. What are the human needs? To love and be loved; to be supported, sheltered, and protected; to be heard, honored, and accepted; to be faithful to the other in thought, word, and deed. In other words, to love as Jesus loves. We are to love each other as Christ loves His church. That's a tall order for an imperfect and sin-prone creation, but once again, it is God's original best for each of us.

My heart aches for those of you who do not fall into the category of having scriptural grounds for remarriage. You may feel hurt and even desperate as you see yourself trapped in a loveless and contentious marriage for which you see no hope for change or healing. You long for the marriage that is God's original best.

My humanity wants to gather you all up into a tender embrace and say, "Sweet baby, get out of this relationship before it kills you. Leave that alcoholic while he's passed out in the yard; flee from that abusive anger; escape his pornography addiction before it pollutes your children." And then if you say to me, "Can I remarry?" I'd have to say, "Check the Scriptures."

Though God's laws about divorce and remarriage can seem inflexible and demanding, we must always counter His law with His grace. Because God knows we can never live up to His perfect standard, He provides His perfect grace. What does that mean? What I cannot do, He gives me strength to do. He becomes my faithfulness. God says in Ezekiel 36:26–27:

> "I will give you a new heart and put a new spirit within you; I will take the heart of stone out of your flesh and give you a heart of flesh. I will put My Spirit within you and cause you to walk in My statutes, and you will keep My judgments and do them."

Grace means it's not about what we can do, but about what God does because of His love for us. God says He will cause us to live a godly lifestyle. When grace overpowers us, we experience God's faithfulness. What my humanity fails to do, His empowerment accomplishes. Every one of us who reads those words desperately needs an empowerment beyond what our humanity can scrunch up. We all flounder in defeat without the sustaining love and grace of God.

If you are struggling with the consequences of divorce and the longing to do it right the next time, remember:

> The LORD says, "I will guide you along the best pathway for your life. I will advise you and watch over you."
> (Ps. 32:8 NLT)

> The LORD hears his people when they call to him for help. He rescues them from all their troubles.
> (Ps. 34:17 NLT)

> I am overcome with joy because of your unfailing love, for you have seen my troubles, and you care about the anguish of my soul.
> (Ps. 31:7 NLT)

If you do not rest in the arms of another on this earth, you know you will literally rest in the arms of God your Father for all eternity. That may feel like "pie in the sky for the sweet bye and bye" for those of you who don't want to wait that long. Be patient. Since I made the decision to wait for the eternal hug, I'm occasionally reminded of James 4:14, which says, "For what is your life? It is even a vapor that appears for a little time and then vanishes away."

Your next hug may be only a vapor away.

If you do not rest in the arms of another on this earth, you know you will literally rest in the arms of God your Father for all eternity.

ELEVEN

WHAT ABOUT THE KIDS?

> "He will turn the hearts of the fathers to their children, and he will change disobedient minds to accept godly wisdom."
>
> —Luke 1:17 NLT

Some of the most challenging relationships we will ever form are those we develop with our children. Let's look at this letter from the mother of a teenage daughter.

Dear Marilyn,

Do you tell your child the specific reason you divorced, and if so, at what age? I have a daughter from my first marriage. The marriage lasted eight years, and we divorced when our daughter was two due to his repeated infidelity. He left me when I was pregnant. We were separated, and he had two affairs (one with his best friend's wife). We reconciled after our child was born. I gave it my best and prayed all the time that "my marriage would work/get better." When I caught him at it again, I knew it was time to move on. I realized later that I should have been praying for God's will to be done.

Following the divorce, I was given sole physical custody of our daughter, and we shared legal custody. As my daughter approached her middle school years, she began struggling with the absence of her father, who lived two thousand miles away. Once he remarried, his visits became less frequent. She resented my new husband, and we began observing defiant behavior. This evolved into mood swings and anorexia. My twelve-year-old daughter went from eighty pounds to forty-two pounds in six months. To make a long story short, by the time she was fourteen years of age, her medical providers advised that she either check in to a residential treatment facility or go live with her father. I went with what I hoped would be best for her.

She's been living with her father for sixteen months now and is healthy and back to a normal weight.

In the last two years, she has asked me twice why her father and I divorced. Once she even inquired if a third party was involved. Since that was on Christmas Eve, I responded that I would be happy to have an open and honest discussion with her but not on Christmas Eve. Shortly after, she informed me that she didn't want to know anymore.

She is now fifteen years old and a sophomore in high school. Do I tell her the details next time she asks? Should I just bring it up? Or do I just continue to keep the ugly details to myself? Of course, my parents think she should know the entire story, because then she would move back home to live with me. (They haven't forgiven and moved on. I had to.) I just want to do what is best for my daughter.

—Wanting What's Best

I commend you for doing what's best for your daughter. Your parents are reacting out of understandable loyalty to you and equally understandable anger at their cheatin' son-in-law. The mistake many parents make is to diminish anything of value the ex-husband (or wife) has to offer as a parent. When that ex-husband is criticized, ridiculed, or made to sound worthless, the child is put in an awkward position of having to choose. The child feels guilty for loving her daddy, because it feels as if she's being disloyal to Mom. So the child tries to ride the fence. That is an enormous tension the child should be spared.

Actually, you want to be praising your daughter's

father as much as possible. She is 50 percent of his gene pool, and if he's described as a jerk, your daughter may assume she's one too. I realize giving praise to a guy with your ex-husband's track record is an enormous stretch, but you aren't doing the praise talk for his personal benefit. You're doing it for your daughter's.

Your question of how much and when to tell your daughter why you are no longer married to her dad is, of course, a very sensitive issue. Something shut her down, since she says she doesn't want to know anything now. That really is not true, but either she's gone into hiding on the issue or been told information that may or may not be accurate. Whatever the case may be, I suggest you keep the ugly details to yourself. Perhaps the day will come when she can be told her dad simply chose not to stay in the marriage any longer. But remember, you want to preserve her sense of stability and well-being. You do not want to put the ugly load on her. It wasn't her fault, but she may still feel responsible, even though that does not make sense. Even grown-up kids often wonder if "it" was something they did or did not do.

How much marital "junk" to share with the kids is a challenging issue. Consider the following question.

Dear Marilyn,

My parents divorced when I was in my early teens. At the time of my graduation, my mom told me the truth behind the breakup. I learned that my dad was bisexual and leaning more and more toward homosexual. I also learned much later in life that he molested both of my brothers. I know my older brother forgave him long ago (our dad has been deceased for some years). I have long forgiven him, but my question is how to share this information with my two daughters, eighteen and twenty. Because they never met him, their questions are few and far between. They know most everything about our family but not this part. Is it okay to just leave it be?

—Buried Past

Of what benefit would it be to tell your daughters? This information is about a grandfather who was never a part of their lives. I imagine they have little if any interest in the details of his world. If he were still living and had access to their children, then his behavior would need to be communicated. Under the circumstances, I suggest you remain silent. You are not being dishonest. You are merely being discreet.

These last two letters underscore a basic truth: life is messy. The degree of messy is very often the result of our choices—the good ones gone bad and the bad ones staying bad or getting worse. But often we have no way of anticipating a good one going bad. We make a decision based on available information and then move forward.

For example, this woman who divorced her husband because he was bisexual and "leaning more and more toward homosexual," probably had no prior knowledge of her husband's deeper inclinations when she married him. We can probably assume she married in good faith, with the happy expectation that her marriage would be good and her children healthy and happy—the "normal" goals of life. However, her goals and expectations were shattered. The horror of her husband molesting their two sons is mind-boggling. Was she in any way responsible for this messy and heartbreaking turn of events? From the little information we receive from the daughter's question to me, her mother made what she thought was a good marital choice, but it went bad. It got really messy. That "messy" splashed all over her children, and they became victims.

Here's another messy circumstance that breaks the heart.

The following question is also a heartbreaker.

Dear Marilyn,

How does a divorced mom keep her peace and trust that her only son will make it through school and life if he continually sabotages himself by not handing in assignments and lying about such things? This has been going on since grammar school, and he is now in the tenth grade and getting worse, not better. I pray for him, lift him up to God, rebuke demons, etc., and still nothing. Before you think I haven't done anything else, all this is after the yelling, fighting, tutoring, punishing, banning, etc. I believe by faith that my son will prosper. That is God's promise to me and my future generations. Still, I continually struggle with this faith every time his report card or interim reports come out.

—At My Wits' End

Sweet baby, it sounds like you may have one angry little kid doing his best to punish you for whatever his pain and hurt is about. Did his behavior begin when the marital problems escalated into your divorce some years ago? I realize a tenth grader isn't really a "little kid," but his behavior is that of a child who's hoppin' mad about how things are in his life. Obviously, "yelling, fighting, tutoring, punishing, banning" are not working. Those methods only make him madder and more determined to put you into orbit. They're working for him but not for you. That being the case, you'd be smart to change tactics. I'd suggest a system based on rewards rather than punishment.

Since he's a tenth grader, I assume he's going to want a car eventually. Could you discuss with him what he would like in a car—make, color, year, etc.—and agree to the terms for him earning it? Bring him into this discussion. Tell him you realize you haven't really been on the same page for a lot of years, and you are troubled by that. Tell him you want to build a trust between the two of you. The same requirements will exist (school assignments turned in, courteous behavior and cooperation expected), but he will get a cash reward for certain instances of good behavior. Those cash rewards can mount up for the eventual purchase of a car. If he drops the ball, you're not yelling at him. He simply forfeits that reward. Take out a savings account in his name but make sure no money can be withdrawn without your signature. Have him keep the savings account book, and let him watch the money grow or drop, depending on what he does.

Also, since his anger is so intense, zero in on how things were for him prior to the divorce. What did he witness between you and your ex-husband—yelling, shoving, hitting, and the like? How was he treated? Did he feel like a needless piece of furniture you'd rather give to Goodwill than keep around? How is his relationship with his dad now? Does he see him? How does Dad treat him? I'd like to see him find a male role model whose values are Christian and whose heart is expansive toward your son.

My fear is that your son does not feel he matters. I'd also suggest you zero in on him—see the good things he does. Compliment him. Affirm him and demonstrate your love for him. If he is known only for his "sabotage" behavior, it will continue to be a habit. Try to break the habit by little love acts toward him— his favorite ice cream in the freezer, a new CD you know he wants, cooking his favorite dinner, and so on. He needs to feel special.

Do you remember the little poem (that has probably been on every greeting card since 1942) that says, "Love is the answer that everyone seeks—love is the language every heart speaks"? Though the

> *Every heart craves love.*
> *We were created for love.*
> *As you start speaking the*
> *language of love to your*
> *son, I think you'll find*
> *he has ears to hear.*

words are a teensy bit corny, they are totally true! Every heart craves love. We were created for love. As you start speaking the language of love to your son, I think you'll find he has ears to hear.

While many families struggle with parent-child conflict, conflict between siblings can also be difficult and even devastating.

Dear Marilyn,

What do you do with a very stubborn nine-year-old boy that does not like his seven-year-old sister?

143

He also has a three-year-old sister that he loves to bits. For some reason he hates his seven-year-old sister and will do anything to hurt her. How do I stop this terrible rivalry? I don't want it to turn out like Cain and Abel.

—Rivalry Referee

One of the longings we carry with us for a lifetime is for our children to be happy and healthy and to love each other. One of the greatest challenges in many families is sibling rivalry. We often comfort ourselves by saying, "All kids fight, take each other's stuff, and delight in making each other miserable." To varying degrees that is true, and usually the kid stuff works itself out by adulthood (though our longing is for it to work itself out by this afternoon). However, I take the sibling rivalry stuff very seriously, because great emotional damage can be experienced between siblings. Often the parents don't even know it. Parents need to think about this dynamic and realize the potential safety threats that may exist for the child.

Insightfully, you bring up the Cain and Abel story from Genesis 4. Let's remind ourselves of the details surrounding those two siblings.

When they grew up, Abel became a shepherd, while Cain was a farmer. At harvesttime Cain brought to the LORD a gift of his farm produce, while Abel brought several choice lambs from the best of his flock. The LORD accepted Abel and his offering, but he did not accept Cain and his offering. This made Cain very angry and dejected. (vv.2–5 NLT)

Why didn't God accept Cain's offering? Because Cain gave a casual, somewhat meaningless gift to the God who gave Cain life and demanded a life sacrifice in return. When Cain offered a few zucchini, onions, and beets, God rejected the produce. The purpose of bringing God sacrifices was to demonstrate reverence and gratitude for God's gifts. A sacrifice had to be one of shed blood. That sounds a bit gross, but blood is the consistent biblical symbol of the offering of one's life. Abel reached out toward God by giving Him the substitute blood of a lamb. Cain blew the offering off with a few onions.

Genesis 4:6 tells us God's response to Cain: "Why are you so angry? Why do you look so dejected?"(NLT). God goes on to instruct him about how to gain God's favor: "You will be accepted if you respond in the right way. But if you refuse to respond correctly, then watch out! Sin is waiting to attack and destroy you, and you must subdue it" (Gen. 4:7 NLT).

Cain does not take God's instruction and instead takes Abel out into a field and kills him. After Cain is banished to become a "homeless fugitive on the earth" (Gen. 4:12 NLT) as punishment for his sin, Cain whines to God saying, "My punishment is too great for me to bear!" (v. 13 NLT).

In the Genesis 4:6–7 passage, we have our first look at what God models for us as parents when child discipline is called for. Let's examine the principles God used with Cain and apply them to us as parents:

1. Listen to the child.
2. Having listened, communicate how to make things right.
3. Give a warning: state the consequences if the behavior does not change.
4. If the behavior does not change, do what you said you'd do.
5. Ignore subsequent whining; don't back down.

Let's return now to the specifics of your question. You say, "For some reason he hates his seven-year-old sister and will do anything to hurt her," and I've suggested you pay close attention to this dynamic. Take it seriously and watch it closely. Hurting his sister is not allowed—ever. He will need consistent discipline regarding his behavior toward her. You, of course, have a special mandate to protect her from his anger and possible abuse.

In trying to figure out your son's motivation for hating one sister and loving the other, go back and replay the circumstances of the seven-year-old's birth. She basically "dethroned" her brother who had, until then, been King Baby. Do you remember if everyone made a fuss over new baby sister and temporarily did not notice baby brother? A dear friend of mine told me that when her twin sisters were born, she felt totally erased from the planet. She was two years old and no longer Queen Baby. She told me she used to stare into their little twin bassinettes and plot how to get rid of them. She thought maybe she might be able to sell them but couldn't figure out how to do that without Mama noticing. Now they are very close and love each other enormously. But my friend said it was years before she got over the emotional intrusion of their births. They totally changed her position in the family.

So now what? If there is something to the King Baby hunch, what should you be doing? I think the role of your husband is crucial here. Your son needs to witness proper treatment of "women," even if they are only three and seven years old. He needs to learn they are to be protected and respected. If your son does not cooperate with this training, he needs to experience consequences, which your husband should administer. I suggest your son and his dad have special outings—outings only the "men" get to do: camping, fishing, bumper-car rides, basketball games, and so on. This may help your son to feel it's a good thing to be a boy and that he did not really lose as much as he thought when he was toppled from his throne.

Since We're Chatting . . .

I hate the fact that there were far too many times I was a selfish mom. It hurts my heart to remember how many times what I needed to do took precedence over what my kids needed me to do. Like the time I needed to correct at least twenty more essays before I made dinner by six o'clock, even though ten-year-old Jeff needed to go to the tropical fish store before they closed at six o'clock. How could getting a new angelfish be more important than correcting freshman comp papers and making a meat loaf?

All too often the meat loaf won. Now, who cares? Who remembers? The kids do. They may not remember the fish or the meat loaf, but the soul imprint leaves a memory trace. That memory trace weaves back to other times when Mom's "to do" list took precedence over theirs. If that happens too frequently with a child, his or her sense of personal value suffers. The inner message is *I'm really not very important. I need to have fewer needs.*

Of course, we need to strike a balance with kids. Some seem to rule the roost, while others aren't sure where the roost is or if it will change by next weekend. Both extremes cause insecurity. The bottom line: kids need to know they matter. They do not need to be in charge, nor should they be in charge. They simply need to know they are enormously important and consistently loved by their parents.

The kids suffer the greatest fallout when the relationship between Mom and Dad skids into the ditch. They have lost their footing. They spend time worrying if it was their fault. They also hear the continual murmuring of questions: "What about me? Where do I belong? Where will I live? Will I still be loved?"

> *The bottom line: kids need to know they matter. They do not need to be in charge . . . They simply need to know they are enormously important and consistently loved by their parents.*

A new marriage presents more murmuring questions: Why does Mom's new husband like his daughter more than he likes me? Why can't I have my own room? Sometimes Mom doesn't seem to even see me—where did she go? Does she love me like she used to? Is she really happy? Should I be helping? I don't like the man she married. I miss my dad. I don't like the woman he married either. He doesn't notice me much anymore. Is he finally happy? Has he stopped yelling? He was supposed to pick me up from school yesterday—why didn't he ever come? I feel scared all the time.

We frequently hear the phrase, "Kids are resilient—they'll survive." The strongest instinct in all human beings is the survival instinct; it is a primal instinct that takes precedence over all others. So, yes, kids generally survive. The more important question is, do they thrive? Frequently they do not. They develop various coping methods meant to ensure their survival: drugs, alcohol, sex, self-mutilation, eating disorders, and other addictions.

Though this all sounds pretty bleak, the key to reversing destructive coping mechanisms is consistent love. Our kids need to be loved not indulged, affirmed not ignored. They ultimately need to understand that sometimes moms and dads simply can't mend the marriage. That is a less-than-perfect situation the kids will one day need to wrap their minds and emotions around.

But for now and for always, they need to know the deep commitment of parental love that will never desert them, never walk away, never be misplaced or forgotten. That's "Jesus love." They need Jesus love modeled by you. They need your Jesus kind of love slathered all over them.

TWELVE

FACING THE GROTESQUE

> *So God let them go ahead and do whatever shameful things their hearts desired. As a result, they did vile and degrading things with each other's bodies.*
>
> —*Romans 1:24* NLT

Southern writer Flannery O'Connor admits to a childhood fascination with malformed chickens. She said she favored those with one green eye or over-long necks and crooked combs. She always wanted a chicken with three legs or three wings but never had the good fortune of finding one.

I loved teaching Flannery O'Connor, although initially nearly all my students found her writing offensive. Her fiction is filled with bizarre situations and grotesque characters whose behavior may at first be wryly humorous, but then the action turns to startling and unexpected violence.

For example, the character Manley Pointer in the short story "Good Country People" is a Bible salesman who goes from door to door in rural communities claiming he wants to do good. He's described as not a bad-looking young man, wearing a bright blue suit and yellow socks that appear to be continually sucked up by his shoes.

The character Hulga is a bitter woman in her thirties with a PhD in philosophy and a wooden leg. She lost her leg in a hunting accident, was fitted with a wooden one, and has been clumping about the house as loudly as possible to annoy her mother ever since. Manley is fascinated by her atheism as well as her wooden leg. Hulga decides to seduce him to prove her own superiority and to see him reduced to the fool she considers him to be.

During that seduction scene, Manley unhooks her leg while gulping whiskey from a flask in a hollow Bible at the bottom of his suitcase. He then stuffs the leg into his suitcase and makes preparations to leave. She screams at him to return her leg and says that he's the same kind of Christian she's always known: a liar and a hypocrite. He shouts back at her saying she ain't so smart, 'cause he's been believing in nothing ever since he was born. With that he exits the barn and hits the dusty road with more Bibles to sell.

O'Connor claimed to be absorbed by many of the chief mysteries of the Christian life. She was especially interested in faith and the many layers of human deceit that wrap themselves around faith. Most of O'Connor's characters don't see their faith as phony until forced to look at it through a new lens of understanding. That new look comes as a result of a jolting, startling, or even weird circumstance somewhere in the story line.

Manley has never had any faith, but that has nothing to do with selling Bibles. There is money in selling Bibles. Faith in what he sells is of no consequence to him. Hulga claims never to have had faith because it defies logic. Everything of consequence is filtered through her mind, and faith gets stuck in the filter.

Oddly enough, in this story, the faith issue centers around the possession of Hulga's wooden leg. Manley is fascinated by it, and Hulga uses it as a lure. In the end, Manley makes off with the leg, still proclaiming his lack of faith, while Hulga screams that he's just another hypocrite. However, unexpectedly, she says to his retreating figure, "I thought you were just good country people." For a moment, Hulga was putting her faith in the faith of the Bible salesman. The leg is the grotesque symbol of misplaced faith. Manley chooses it and runs with it rather than being "good country people."

"Well," you say. "Marilyn, what's this little literary bit about? What in the world does it have to do with the subject of this chapter, and why would you gross me out with that stupid wooden leg?" Here's what it's about: literature mirrors life. Sometimes literature reflects the sweet "boy meets girl, girl falls in love, girl has pretty clothes" side of life. But if literature is to reflect life in its less attractive, less compelling states, it has to show the underbelly side of life.

What O'Connor forces the reader to do is look at the weird, the ugly, the grotesque, and the unthinkable. Why does she do that? Why should we read it? Most of us don't want to see the weird and the ugly. But sometimes life is messy, and we must look at it whether we want to or not.

To me, the most grotesque and unthinkable experience in life is sexual abuse. I can hardly stand to think about it. I hate even knowing it exists. But it does exist. In fact, Women of Faith sent out questionnaires to hundreds of you, asking you to tell me your areas of concern so that I could respond to them and write this book. The greatest number of questions I received in response had to do with sexual abuse. The deepest heartache I heard was from those upon whom sexual abuse has cast a huge shadow. I have felt honored to be drawn into your hurting places. I feel honored that you trust me enough to lift the curtain shrouding the place of your pain—that you believe I may be able to throw some light into those dark corners.

And so, dear ones, we'll consider this subject, quote your letters, and claim God's hope, healing, and restoration for every single one of you. In so doing, we will remember the fantastic promise from 1 John 4:4, "Because the Spirit who lives in you is greater than the spirit who lives in the world" (NLT). We are not fighting a losing battle. This battle is against the worst form of evil. It is an ugly, palpitating pain, and I'm convinced it originates straight from the pit of hell. Yet God reminded His people, who felt overwhelmed and afraid in the face of the enemy, "The battle is not yours but God's" (2 Chron. 20:15 NLT). This enemy is utterly demonic, but God does not leave us alone in the fight. Second Timothy 4:18 states, "And the Lord will deliver me from every evil work and preserve me for His heavenly kingdom."

Of course, the question so frequently asked is, why does God allow this kind of evil? Since the promise is to "deliver me from every evil work," why not prevent that evil work from ever happening in the first place?

God seems to place a high priority on the right of individuals to choose good or evil. That right extended to the angel kingdom as well. Satan became restless with his status as an angel. He was ambitious. He wanted more. More what? Power and glory. In fact, Satan wanted God's power and glory. Satan wanted to be God. Satan began a grumble campaign among the other angels who agreed with Satan's assessment that God is too powerful. They rebelled against the hierarchy of God. God allowed that rebellious choice to be made. They decided to do evil against God and His creation. The result? A battleground on earth. Ephesians 6:12 describes that battleground:

> For we do not wrestle against flesh and blood, but against principalities, against powers, against the rulers of the darkness of this age, against spiritual hosts of wickedness in the heavenly places.

God does not dictate our choices. Were He to prevent evil, He would be going against His established order—the right to choose between good and evil. When evil is chosen, the consequences of that choice often fall upon the unsuspecting and the innocent. That seems unfair and unjust to us. Why should the innocent suffer? The suffering of the innocent is appalling to us. But the suffering of the innocent is part of the fallout of the original choice Adam and Eve made in the garden to disobey God. He allowed their choice; we experience its consequence.

Could God put a stop to all evil? Of course. Could He prevent sexual abuse? Yes. But in preventing one evil, He must then prevent all evil. That would be a world without sin. Unfortunately, sin was chosen. God allowed that choice to be made.

Our choice now is to realize a battle is going on. We choose not to be defeated in that battle. Jesus called Satan a liar—the father of all lies (John 8:44). Satan's greatest lie to the abuse victim is, "God does not love you. He does not care about you. If He did, you would not have experienced what you did." God does care. His heart is always grieved when one of His children is hurt. His intent is to cast light into the darkest of lies and gently lead us into that place of trusting His word of love for us.

The following question expresses so well how difficult it is to understand that God does indeed love us but allows that which feels as if it could destroy us.

Dear Marilyn,

I am a fifty-eight-year-old mother of two adult children and grandmother to a fourteen-year-old girl and nine-year-old boy. I am a believer whose faith is deeply grounded. It was shaken and put to the test when I discovered that my granddaughter, now fourteen, was raped and molested by her stepfather almost every weekday from the time she was six until she was twelve. We suspect that my grandson was probably molested, but he won't talk about it.

Having been brought up in a Christian home where church was a priority every time the doors were open, I was taught that the world is full of evil because Satan roams, looking to destroy lives, and he especially loves to destroy the testimony and faith of believers. I have accepted that truth for my entire life. As a minister, I have counseled women on the difficulty of understanding why God allows such things. I have spent years trying to answer the unanswerable questions, trying to help young women who have suffered much to hang on to their faith.

It has been two years and unending therapy since my daughter and I discovered these atrocities. My daughter still hates this man—all men. My granddaughter has done little healing and trusts absolutely no one. My grandson is trying to cope with what he knows or may have dealt with. To this day, as much as I love God, as much as I follow Jesus, as much as I cling to the Holy Spirit who comforts me, I am often overcome with feelings of deep anger, grief, disappointment, unforgiveness, and a huge question mark in my heart. I don't love God less, and I want to say I don't trust Him less. But deep in my being I wonder how and why a God who creates such beauty, who loves immeasurably, who knows all things, who sacrificed his own Son for us, would create a being who would perpetuate such evil. How do I reconcile that within myself so that I can look in the faces of the women whose children have been harmed, disfigured, diseased, or born dead, or who have themselves suffered physical or sexual abuse, and exclaim with the strongest faith that God has a plan and that all things work together for good.

—Deeply Saddened

Romans 8:28 is a familiar and much-needed verse. It assures us that good can come from bad. But the verse doesn't tell us *how* good comes from bad, only that it does. Let's review it. "We know that all things work together for good to those who love God, to those who are the called according to His purpose" (Rom. 8:28).

Obviously, our circumstances don't always change and become good. We would like to twist that verse around to guarantee us a tangible good, but that may not always happen. What does happen is that God can take that bad and weave it into the fabric of our lives, bringing ultimate victory, increased faith, and a pervading peace. In fact, that is always His intent.

The phrase "my granddaughter has done little healing and trusts absolutely no one" is a heartbreaker. On the human level, it is so easy to understand her feelings. She has been violated. Her trust has been wrenched from her, and she is left with the emptiness that accompanies the loss of trust. You, the grandmother, can't imagine why such soul devastation was allowed. It is unthinkable. It is grotesque. I could not agree more.

In the face of such evil, what do we do? What is our choice? We can buy into the lie of Satan that God could not possibly care, or we can fight like mad and refuse the lie. When we do that, we have entered into spiritual battle. Here's the battle promise:

> Can anything ever separate us from Christ's love? Does it mean he no longer loves us if we have trouble or calamity, or are persecuted, or are hungry or cold or in danger or threatened with death? . . . No, despite all these things, overwhelming victory is ours through Christ, who loved us. (Rom. 8:35–37 NLT)

According to this verse, here's the bottom line for you, dear writer: you and your children are promised victory in the battle. The sustaining love of Christ will never desert you. Your devastating experience did not come into your life because God stopped loving you.

But how do these truths get woven into your life? How do your daughter and granddaughter come to that place of promised victory? That sounds like a huge stretch. Humanly, it is.

I have spent enough years as a mental health professional to believe in the undeniable value of psychological therapy. That you have spent time in "unending therapy" is a good thing—it provided you with labels, tools, catharsis, and a better understanding of your soul wound. At the same time, it can be discouraging; anger, hopelessness, and a lack of trust remain dominant forces for your family. Because sexual abuse can have such a demonic grip on the soul, I firmly believe there are times when prayer for emotional healing needs to be included in the "war package" for victory. I'm not just talking about friends and support groups, but a specific, focused ministry. This ministry reflects training, experience, and an understanding of the overwhelming spiritual challenges to the soul's healing.

Since you are on a church ministerial staff, you may be aware of this type of ministry in your area. The one with which I am the most familiar is called Philippian Ministries, headquartered in Dallas, Texas. The founder and director is a sexual abuse survivor and is well-versed in the journey to wholeness. She never in a million years expected victory. Now she and her organization lead thousands into a new understanding of God's love and His determination to heal. I suggest you research a healing ministry for your daughter and your granddaughter. God will not waste all you've done so far.

Finally, let me remind you of those familiar promises found yet again in Romans 8:

Do you think anyone is going to be able to drive a wedge between us and Christ's love for us? There is no way! Not trouble, not hard times, not hatred, not hunger, not homelessness, not bullying threats, not backstabbing, not even the worst sins listed in Scripture. . . . I'm absolutely convinced that nothing—nothing living or dead, angelic or demonic . . . *nothing* can get between us and God's love. (vv. 35,38–39 MSG).

Dear one, the last chapter of your battle has yet to be written. We both know God is more powerful than the enemy of our souls. Satan hates it when we hurl Scripture at him, so heave away, sweetheart. That's part of the battle plan. And remember that in God's timetable, your victory banners are already waving.

Since We're Chatting . . .

I am aware of a national healing and miracle ministry that assumes sexually abused persons are demon-oppressed. This ministry believes the memories of the abused person are made-up fantasies that in reality never happened. They assume the so-called memories are the lies of a demon living within the victim. The ministry strategy then is to cast out the demons through exorcism.

This is a dangerous misconception of what is meant by the phrase "healing-prayer ministry." A legitimate ministry does not deny the person's history of sexual abuse. It does not relegate memories of that abuse to demons living within the victim. The last thing the abuse victim needs is to be told that the surfacing memories are demon-inspired lies. That causes the victim to retreat back into the safety of denial. I think I might retreat, too, if I thought it would get me out of an exorcism.

Instead, I suggest the addition of a specific prayer person to come alongside the therapeutic process. Years before my Women of Faith era, I counseled in Newport Beach, California. I worked with a dear woman who came to me because of depression. We worked together for several years, and in that time, we realized she had been sexually abused by her grandfather. The pattern of her abuse was not violent or even invasive. He would have her sit on his lap, and she was instructed in how to fondle him. This was their "secret," and he told her if she ever told the secret, it would make her little sister jealous because she had not been "the chosen lap person." This went on several years before her grandfather had a stroke and was put in a rest home. She did not remember ever seeing him again.

When we first started working together, she had no

memories of her abuse. Her memories of her grandfather were hazy, and she felt uncomfortable and guilty when she talked about the little she could remember. She did not know why. Ultimately, when her memories began to surface from the cellar of her mind, she felt incredible grief. The grief was not for herself—the innocent, trusting little girl who sat on her grandfather's lap. Her grief was for her grandfather—his loneliness after his wife died, his loss of freedom in no longer being able to drive, and his memory lapses that made living alone unsafe for him. She also grieved that she had not been able to help him. Did she do something wrong that caused his stroke and his ultimate removal from her house? This false guilt was overwhelming her.

For some reason, my client and I reached an impasse. She could not move away from her feelings of guilt or the defensiveness she felt for her grandfather. In spite of my therapeutic techniques, the logjam remained. She needed to feel empathy for the little girl on the lap. She needed to realize how utterly wrong and unacceptable the behavior of her grandfather was. Instead, she cried for him and not herself.

As I prayed for this client one evening, driving home to Laguna Beach, the Holy Spirit gave me a nudge. Sometimes it takes me a while to recognize the holy nudge, but this one I got immediately. I was nudged to suggest to my client that she pray with a woman whose prayer ministry I deeply respected. I had known her to "pray through" some extremely difficult spiritual challenges in my church. This woman would be balanced, intelligent, and sensitive to the things of the Spirit. Quite frankly, I think my professional ego was a little bruised that the logjam existed in my client and my methods were not causing the jam to break up. Putting my ego aside, my client seemed eager to pray with my suggested intercessor. An appointment was set up immediately. For one full day, they prayed together, talked together, and watched the waves of the ocean crashing to the shore beneath the intercessor's cedar deck. By four o'clock that afternoon, there was peace. The Spirit of God intervened, and my client saw herself held lovingly in the arms of her Father, safe from all the crashing waves and free from all the false accusations. Healing occurred that day. The logjam broke up. She came to see her grieving was more a longing for her absent daddy than a defense of her ever-present grandfather.

That experience reminded me again that God is utterly creative and totally faithful. I was not chosen to facilitate that healing for my client in Laguna Beach. Thank God, we can trust Him to know when and how to heal. I am continually amazed at His style. I am also quieted by the pervasive love He provides to all of us, His children.

THIRTEEN

FORGIVING AND FORGETTING

> *"If you forgive others, you will be forgiven."*
> —*Luke 6:37* NLT

One of the hardest things to do is to forgive someone for inflicting pain we don't believe we deserve. Why *should* a person who inflicts pain on another be forgiven? It does not make sense to us. The following question is very natural.

Dear Marilyn,

As a child I was sexually and verbally abused by my parents. Many people are telling me I need to forgive. This seems impossible. It's not like they bumped my car in a parking lot.

—Still Hurt

Still Hurt uses familiar logic. If the offense were simply bumping her car in a parking lot, it would be easier to forgive her parents. But what they did was far more painful. They robbed her of her trust, innocence, security, value, and future as a functioning sexual being. We believe that the bigger the offense, the harder it is to forgive. Do we ever have a justification not to forgive? Are not some sins too terrible to merit forgiveness? I think so. But God doesn't. So I can't operate out of my human inclination to mow down every sex offender with my eighteen-wheeler. That would be my way. That would never be God's way.

What's so wrong with my eighteen-wheeler solution? Not only is that solution totally out of sync with how God operates, but it is also totally out of sync with what is best for me. As much as I may relish thoughts of human revenge, those vengeful thoughts and images put me in a dark place.

> *Are not some sins too terrible to merit forgiveness? I think so. But God doesn't.*

God does not want me in that dark place. When I stand in that dark place, my soul shrivels. What does a shriveled soul look like? It wallows in:

negativity

bitterness

resentment

depression

insomnia

eating disorders

addictions

suicidal inclinations

Isaiah 2:5 says to me, "Let us walk in the light of the LORD!" (NLT). First John 1:5–6 also boots me along with these words: "God is light and in Him is no darkness at all. If we say that we have fellowship with Him, and walk in darkness, we lie and do not practice the truth."

A lack of forgiveness puts us in spiritual darkness no matter how understandable our inability to forgive. We suffer in that darkness. Forgiveness benefits us not only because it is an act of obedience to God but also because it frees us from the bitterness that would keep us in the dark with an increasingly shriveled soul. For this reason, Jesus taught that we are to love our enemies. He also said, "Pray for those who persecute you!" (Matt. 5:44 NLT). Jesus said that when we do pray, we "will be acting as true children" of our Father (Matt. 5:45 NLT).

You, dear writer, do need to forgive your parents. From our human viewpoint, they may not deserve your forgiveness, but you deserve the spiritual light that envelops you when you forgive the unforgivable.

Not only are we to forgive, be we are also to pray for

those who have abused us. That does not mean you have to pray *with* your abuser, but *for* your abuser. Prayer and forgiveness will soften your spirit and ward off the resentment that is always lurking about, wanting to pounce. Interestingly, praying aloud for those who have hurt you can be of even greater benefit for your soul. When we utilize our senses—my voice saying the words, my ears hearing the words—we participate in our own prayer on a deeper level. It's as if the emotions, the words, and the sounds need to get outside of us. In so doing, the forgiveness experience and the increased prayerful attitude become a greater reality to the various dimensions of our internal being.

Our minds also benefit from forgiveness. How we think determines how we feel. When we think negative thoughts, we're going to feel negative emotions. That's not good for us. First Peter 3:8 reminds us, "All of you should be of one mind, full of sympathy toward each other, loving one another with tender hearts and humble minds" (NLT). Thoughts of sympathy and tenderness toward those who have hurt us seem an enormous stretch. I know it is not possible without divine enablement, but we can ask God for that enablement. We can pray that we will be enabled to pray; we can pray that we will be enabled to receive the mind of Christ as we pray. The mind of Christ is of great benefit to all of us. He offers it. We need it. We can choose to receive it.

Even as I write these paragraphs, I am aware that many of you may still be trembling on the brink of healing from abuse. The very thought of praying for that person may cause you to run into the familiar darkness of denial, saying, "I can't do that! Are you crazy?" I admit it sounds impossibly crazy to pray for someone who has dishonored and demeaned you. Prayer for your abuser may be years down the healing path for you. What God would have us understand in this process of healing is that He knows we, His treasured creatures, are frail and exceedingly fragile. He will not ask more of us than we are able to do. What we are able to do comes only from Him anyway. So take the necessary time, dear ones, and be encouraged by this lifetime guarantee:

> "I created you and have cared for you since before you were born. I will be your God throughout your lifetime—until your hair is white with age. I made you, and I will care for you. I will carry you along and save you." (Isa. 46:3–4 NLT)

With the benefits of forgiveness in mind, let's now turn to what so frequently confuses us: how forgiveness operates. What does it look like, and how can we know if we truly have forgiven? If we forgive, does that mean we also need to forget the offense? Consider the following letter.

Dear Marilyn,

I am a well-adjusted forty-seven-year-old woman who was sexually, physically, and mentally abused as a child by my father. Over the years, I learned to love myself as God loves me. My question is this—my mother and father both have admitted the abuse but have never said they were sorry or asked for my forgiveness. We have not spoken in over fifteen years. As a Christian, I felt that I should forgive them as God forgave me by dying on the cross. I don't blame them, but how do I honestly forgive them? I want to forgive them, and I have even written them a letter (which went unanswered) telling them that I forgave them and that I pray for their salvation. But how do I deal with the feelings I get every now and then of anger toward them for what they did? If I have forgiven them, how do I forgive and forget? Does any of this make sense? I love Jesus with all my heart, and I live my life the way I believe Jesus would want me to.

—Forgive and Forget

You, sweet baby, are to be commended! You have reached a place of no longer blaming them for your lost childhood. That in itself is a giant step in your forgiveness experience. You understand they are mentally sick individuals. You wrote them a letter telling them you've forgiven them. Whether they answered or not, you are in the clear simply by writing to them. And now, the next step you need to realize is that forgiving and forgetting are not the same. I doubt you will ever forget what they did to you, but you need to know you are not required to forget it. Let's talk about the difference between forgiving and forgetting.

To forgive is to excuse or pardon. The person who receives forgiveness is free from making any kind of payment for that forgiven offense. God forgives us of all confessed sin. The required payment for sin is death. Jesus did that for us. We do not pay the penalty for our sin.

You, dear writer, have lifted the penalty from your parents for their sin against you. Nothing but their choice of believing and receiving Jesus will lift or remove their sin against God. The fact that you are not trying to figure out ways to punish your parents is an indication that you truly have forgiven them.

So now, what about forgetting? Frequently, the verses about God forgetting our sins are interpreted as meaning our sins are no longer known by Him—as if there is some kind of amnesia God squirts over His memory. It's as if our sin is beyond His ability to recall. It's important for us to remember that God uses human terminology to explain a heavenly reality. God's memory of our sin shows that the penalty for that sin has been paid. There is no point in fretting over something that no longer requires payment. When God says He remembers our sin no more, it means He remembers it against us no more. If you are trying to forget your parents' sin against you, as God does, simply remember you are no longer holding their sin against them. You will always remember the events, but forgiveness allows you to be free from the crippling consequences of an unforgiving spirit.

Even when you have occasional bursts of anger, you can fight those memories by saying, "In Jesus' name, I've forgiven you." The enemy loses his power over you when you say the name of Jesus. Your parents' behavior has no more power over you. The name of Jesus is your power source. The fact that you may have need of His name does not mean you have not forgiven. It means you have not forgotten and may need "Jesus power surges" as an enablement to deal with your human frailty. That frailty will dog us all as long as we live. Until we are in heaven, we'll always know we're on earth. Don't be hard on yourself for being human.

There's yet another important thought about forgetting that we need to discuss. Philippians 3:13 is often quoted as a motivator for us to forget our past. Let's review that verse: "No, dear brothers and sisters, I am still not all I should be, but I am focusing all my energies on this one thing: Forgetting the past and looking forward to what lies ahead" (NLT).

Preceding the thirteenth verse, Paul is talking about his degree of zeal as a Jewish scholar and ardent believer.

He speaks of his regret over his leadership in persecuting the new church. Paul is saying that he regards all his religious and academic accomplishments as garbage now that he knows Jesus as his Lord and Savior. He is not literally forgetting his past sins. He is not forgetting his once-coveted status and prestige as a Jewish leader. But he has a new focus and is grateful his past focus will not be held against him. His past is forgiven. The memory of his past causes him to remember the grace of God in forgiving his sin. Memory can inspire little praise services in all of us as we remember what we were saved from.

The fact that your parents "never said they were sorry" or asked for your forgiveness is naturally an added hurt to your already hurting heart. You have explained their behavior to yourself, but there is something in each of us that longs for an apology, an acknowledgment of wrongdoing, an admission of guilt. Proverbs 18:20 says, "Words satisfy the soul as food satisfies the stomach; the right words on a person's lips bring satisfaction" (NLT). You may never hear those right words. I am so sorry. You deserve words of apology, but you also deserve to be free of your parents' toxicity. In your mind, do as Paul did. Remember, but know that remembering need not distort your focus on what lies ahead. It encourages you to move ahead.

Since We're Chatting . . .

There is a side of the forgiveness process that concerns me, one that is often misunderstood. It is raised in the following question.

> Dear Marilyn,
>
> I am the victim of childhood sexual abuse by my oldest brother. I am now married, and within days of giving birth to my son, I was struck with a severe case of postpartum depression. After a year of counseling and medication, I came to understand that much of my breakdown was attributable to my abuse as a child, and I began a relationship with Christ. My husband and I cut off all contact with my brother. We both agree we do not want our son to be in danger, so he has never met his uncle. I believe forgiveness is the answer, but can I have forgiveness but still no relationship with him?
>
> —Broken Trust

It's unfortunate, but to cut off contact with your brother to ensure your son's safety is wisdom. Your son's well-being is your first responsibility. You are not attempting to punish your brother. You are protecting a precious life God has entrusted to you.

I believe it is possible to forgive someone and have nothing whatever to do with him. A relationship is always built on trust. The trust in your relationship with your brother was shattered by his own doing. It was his decision to violate your innocence, take what was never his, trespass the boundary of your human dignity, and reduce you to an object designed for his sexual pleasure. There is no excuse whatever for such behavior under any circumstance at any time. His behavior is inexcusable—but not unforgivable. Though he is totally without excuse, that does not mean he is beyond the grace and forgiveness of God. I may be revving the engine of my eighteen-wheeler, but God is offering love and forgiveness.

Does your brother deserve your forgiveness? God says yes. Based on that knowledge, you can determine—with God's enablement—to forgive your brother. In so doing, you have obeyed God. As we have already discussed, there is great reward when we obey His Spirit and His Word.

But now what do I do? The "now what" depends on how you feel about your brother. If he has apologized sincerely for his sinful behavior and wants to reestablish contact, is there room in your heart for him? If your answer is yes, his job is to begin repairing the trust foundation he shattered. That will take time. You are not responsible for that effort. You are responsible for the act of forgiveness only you can do. He is responsible for the foundation repair only he can do.

Many confuse trust and forgiveness. For example, a wife may truly forgive her husband's infidelity but not yet trust him. That lack of trust does not indicate a lack of forgiveness. The husband needs to patiently build his wife's confidence in him again. He is not automatically restored to his former position.

Similarly, an abusive husband may be forgiven, but that does not mean he's invited to move back into his former home. An abusive father is forgiven, but his child may still feel uncomfortable in his presence. The abuser may have done his part in the restoration process—growing, learning, and developing into a new person whose behavior reflects change—but that process is his, not the victim's. The victim's responsibility is to forgive, not necessarily to receive the former abuser back into her life. This aspect of forgiveness can be liberating for those who live in fear of a return to an unhealthy situation.

FOURTEEN

MANAGING OUR EXPECTATIONS

> *"For I know the plans I have for you," says the* LORD, *"They are plans for good and not for disaster, to give you a future and a hope."*
> —*Jeremiah 29:11* NLT

We're going to change our focus now by returning to a few more general issues that challenge us all in one way or another. As we began this journey together, I suggested that human relationships often influence whether we soar like an eagle or wallow like a hippopotamus. I also pointed to the brilliance of Romans 12:2, "Let God transform you into a new person by changing the way you think" (NLT), as a solution for many of our relational wallowings. If our thinking is out of whack, our behavior will be out of whack. God can help our thinking and behavior by transforming us through His Word. That transformation in turn influences our relationships.

The following letter comes from a hurt and confused young woman who is desperate to mend a broken relationship with her brother. She is in an emotional wallow.

Hi, Marilyn!

I am desperately trying to have a good relationship with my youngest brother, but it just isn't happening. His wife seems to be very controlling and almost seems intent on my brother having little to no contact with his family, though they see her family quite frequently. My brother and I were very close well into our teen years, but ever since they met (he was sixteen at the time and she was twentysomething) and married, our relationship has suffered. They spend a lot of their time in bars, and his wife even dictated the amount of time they spent with my dad when he was dying of cancer. Anytime my mother tries to gently confront my brother, he gets very defensive, and once when Mom suggested she would like to see more of the grandkids, his wife went into a rage, yelling at my mother over how nothing she ever did was good enough. My brother allowed this to happen and only spoke up when Mom told her to stop it, and then he yelled at Mom, telling her not to talk to his wife that

way. I don't know how to approach my brother anymore. What can I do?

—Family Feud

Well, dear writer, it is easy to see why you feel so
hurt by your inability to have a relationship with your
brother. You were once close, but it appears that sweet
bond was severed by the new sister-in-law who insists
her husband have limited time with the members of his
family. It is hard to imagine her dictatorial management
of the time allowed your brother during his dad's fight
with cancer. It is also hard to imagine her yelling at your
mother just because your mother wants time with her
grandchildren. Your brother's wife is totally out of whack.
The only way she seems able to manage her volatile and
fragile emotions is to keep tight control of everything
and everyone.

Your sister-in-law's accusation that "nothing I ever do
is good enough" has a long root that probably stretches
back to childhood. I imagine she was raised to feel
imperfect, not good enough, and that's the lens
through which she sees everything now. Does that
excuse her behavior? Absolutely not. It does, however,
explain her behavior. You are not at fault, and neither
is your mother. There is perhaps some comfort in that
realization.

However, it must be discouraging trying to rebuild

a relationship with your brother when he is being guarded by a Doberman.

Perhaps you need to remind yourself that your brother made a choice. Now he is living out the consequences of that choice. Apparently, he chooses not to take a stand against his wife's unreasonable behavior. He allowed the limited time with his dying father, and he allowed his wife to yell at his mother (not only did he allow it, but he joined in!). He, too, is out of whack.

So where does that leave your relationship with your brother? Penned up! What can you do about it? Apparently very little. Unless your brother chooses to live differently, you will have to rethink your relationship with him. Nothing in the present can rob you of the good memories you have from the past. You will just need to keep those memories separate from the present. Remind yourself that you once had fun times together, and that he is still your brother, but that things are different now.

You need to manage your expectations. Do not let yourself expect what appears to be unrealistic. Does that mean you settle for less? Yes, that's exactly what it means. Unless your sister-in-law gets the professional help she desperately needs, she will continue in her present behavior pattern. Unless your brother decides his wife can no longer dominate him, you will have limited time together.

What Scripture can you claim that will help to transform your thinking? First Peter 2:20 says, "If when you do what is right and suffer for it you patiently endure it, this finds favor with God" (NASB). When you treat your brother and sister-in-law with patience, you are doing what is right. That is not humanly easy, because they are unreasonable. Why should you allow them to get by with unreasonable behavior? You've tried talking gently, and that did not work. Your only option is to back off and be available on their terms. As you do so, remember God asks you to patiently endure. Psalm 34:14 underscores the "patiently endure" suggestion with these words: "Do good; seek peace and pursue it."

Remember this, sweetheart: the last chapter of this experience is not yet written. Leave that to God's sovereignty. In the meantime, choose to live in the peace of His love and creativity. Those "thinkings" will enable you to endure patiently.

Dear Marilyn,

I grew up in a very religious family. From ages four through thirteen I was molested. I was raised to believe that you have to be a virgin when you get married or you're worthless. I lived with so much pain, thinking I would never get married, and also did not want anyone to ever know about my shame. I was welcomed into the homosexual world. They made me feel my past didn't matter there. God set me free from that lifestyle, but now I feel more shame than ever. I really want to be married and have a family, but I can't imagine anyone would want me for a wife. I'm also scared God did not forgive me for that time when I was living like a homosexual.

—Unworthy

Sweet baby, your question breaks my heart. God wants you to know that you were never unworthy of His love. God wants you to know that all confessed sin is forgiven and forgotten. Nothing you have ever done will keep Him from loving you. Nothing you have ever done is beyond His desire to heal.

> *Nothing you have ever done will keep Him from loving you. Nothing you have ever done is beyond His desire to heal.*

The sexual abuse you suffered was not your fault. God would have you stop blaming yourself for that experience. Whoever abused you was at fault. Therefore, it is not your fault that the abuse robbed you of your virginity. God does not see you as one who is unworthy of a loving husband. He sees you as His special treasure, one for whom He has a loving plan.

Remember the sweet promise of Jeremiah 29:11.

"'For I know the plans I have for you,' says the LORD, 'They are plans for good and not for disaster, to give you a future and a hope'" (NLT). That is what God does. Here is what you do, as described in Jeremiah 29:12, "Then you will call upon Me and go and pray to Me, and I will listen to you." You bring to God all your inner torment and shame. Talk to Him, knowing He is not judging you; He is loving you. Even as you talk to Him, He is healing your wounds.

God would also remind you to examine how you are thinking. Psalm 13:2 states, "How long must I wrestle with my thoughts and every day have sorrow in my heart?" (NIV). You must answer that question. You can say, "I am going to stop wrestling with my thoughts of abuse. I am going to stop wrestling with my thoughts of wrongdoing during that homosexual phase. I am going to say yes to God's love and live in His forgiveness."

So now, dear one, know that you are worthy of a husband; you are worthy of having children; you are worthy of the enormous love of the God of the universe. Jesus said in Matthew 10:29–31: "Not even a sparrow, worth only half a penny, can fall to the ground without your Father knowing it. And the very hairs on your head are all numbered. So don't be afraid; you are more valuable to him than a whole flock of sparrows" (NLT). That spiritual truth will transform your thinking and enable some soaring.

Since We're Chatting . . .

You may remember that I advised Family Feud, the sister struggling in her relationship with her brother, that she would be wise to begin managing her expectations. The more she expects their relationship to miraculously return to its past state, the more she will be disappointed and even bitter. Managing our expectations is crucial for all of us; it can prevent us from creeping toward the wallowing hole.

An "expectation" means to look forward to the probable occurrence or appearance of something. I loved watching a realized expectation last week in the Denver airport. A returning soldier from Iraq was received with whoops of joy and delight as his family threw themselves into his arms and buried their faces in his chest. The last to let go was his mama. The family celebrated throughout the terminal and on into the parking lot, where the soldier's truck waited to be driven off by its master. I loved watching it all. And I wondered what the expectations of this young soldier were as he anticipated his two-week visit at home. What I witnessed was the ideal side of his safe return—a waiting, exuberant family, thrilled their loved one had survived the chaos of his time in Iraq. But what followed that exuberance? How did the family dynamic play itself out in the two weeks he was home?

Had those family dynamics changed in the year he had been gone? I found myself speculating as I saw he and his little brother drive off in a new truck, the rest of the family close behind in their own vehicle. Perhaps we could indulge in some imaginings about this soldier's time at home to learn more about our own need to manage expectations.

Perhaps he hoped his mom had gotten over those "little black moods" that caused her to retreat to her bedroom and not come out for several days. Could he expect she had somehow learned to manage those moods and relate in ways that did not create dread for her periodic "black times"? He felt certain he could expect the world's finest fried chicken. No one could fry chicken like his mom. In fact, no one could cook nearly as well as his mom. He expected to eat like a king.

Then there's Dad—his well-intentioned dad who never uttered more than a few sentences a day. Could he expect Dad had come out of his emotional and verbal seclusion in the year of the boy's absence? Before he left for Iraq, Dad handed his son the keys to a brand-new truck, saying merely, "For the day you come home." Had Dad looked away so the tears in his eyes would not be noticed? Did Dad feel more than he ever said? Could the boy expect Dad had learned to show more vulnerability and use words to express it?

And what about his girlfriend? Did she love him as

much now as she did the day he left? Was there a reason he wasn't getting as many letters from her as he had months ago? What could he expect from her as she returned from her first year of college? Had she gotten a new boyfriend? What did he dare expect?

If this fictional account were true, I would want to pull the young soldier aside and tell him that managing his expectations often means lowering them. Mom will probably always make "killer chicken" because she always has. But to expect that she no longer has "black days" is probably unrealistic. Why? Because she has always struggled with dark days. If indeed she had sought professional help for those bouts of darkness, the boy could expect that somehow his mom's chemical balance might have been restored, and he would notice a difference in her ability to cope. That would then become a realistic expectation.

With his nonverbal dad, the boy needs to lower his expectations about Dad's ability to relate. He has always been kind; he has always been dependable; he has never been verbal. It is doubtful he will ever change. That being the case, there is relief in changing expectations, because there's no disappointment when the dad continues to behave as he always has. With that change of expectation comes a measure of security. Dad is who he is. He is a good man. Accept him as he is.

Finally, our soldier needs to ready himself for the possibility that his girlfriend's feelings may have changed. His expectations need to be based on reality. In reality, he has been gone a year, and she's meeting new boys every day. It may be too soon in her young life to commit to a serious, "I'll wait for you forever" relationship. He needs to take into account that in Iraq he is probably not meeting many new faces. This isolation intensifies his need for someone back home. If he is balanced in his expectations of maintaining at least a friendship with his girlfriend, he won't pressure her to meet his overwhelming need.

For this young soldier to manage his expectations, he will need to keep himself in the balance between what he wants and the reality of that which he is likely to receive. That is true for all of us.

One of the cruelest myths that circulates around the "love bubble" is the expectation that now, finally, the person of your dreams has arrived. You are going to marry and live within that bubble of met expectations and tender understandings. Unfortunately, within a very short period of time, the bubble bursts. That does not mean you no longer love the person of your dreams. It means the person of your dreams may watch a lot of football, fall asleep in his recliner every night, and forget to take out the garbage. *Now* is when your expectations for marriage need to be managed. Your husband is not perfect. You, sweet baby, are not perfect. Your house is not perfect; the neighborhood is not perfect . . . The list goes on. So does life.

So what do we do with our expectations? We manage them. In some cases, they need to be lowered. In other cases, they need to be raised. We need to zero in on reality and choose to live within realistic parameters. So often our expectations are not only out of balance in the marriage relationship, but they're also out of balance with our kids. We want the best for them. Actually, we want perfection for them. That is not a realistic expectation. We cannot provide perfection, and they cannot deliver it. So we lower our expectations and accept the fact that the kids next door have the flu and your four-year-old just spent the afternoon at their house.

We must also adjust our expectations about the performances of our kids. Some will be fabulous athletes; some will be average athletes; some will never know what to do with the baseball that falls into their glove. Remembering that giftedness seems at times to skip some families and totally envelop others, we need to adjust our expectations accordingly.

Managing our expectations has nothing whatever to do with negative thinking. It has everything to do with realistic thinking. For example, there was a couple who seemed to be completely on a different page as they discussed the purchase of a new auto. The wife's expectation was for a spiffy little sports car that could zip around traffic. The husband's expectation was for a used car that would be less expensive and more practical. The husband felt his wife was not being financially realistic in her expectation of a sports car. She refused to change her expectations. In their last conversation on the subject, she said, "Look, Walter, just get something fast that can go from 0 to 200 in four seconds or less. My birthday is coming up. Surprise me!" For her birthday, he bought her a brand-new bathroom scale.

While this clever husband makes us laugh, he also demonstrates that our expectations are often unrealistic. Keeping them too high sets us up for disappointment and even resentment in our relationships. So what are we to do? Recognize that nothing is perfect and depend on God to enable us to love as He has called us to love. That love can help us climb out of the wallowing hole to soar like eagles. David expresses the strength, joy, and freedom that follow in Psalm 35:

> But let me run loose and free,
>> celebrating GOD's great work,
> Every bone in my body laughing, singing, "God,
>> there's no one like you."
>
> (vv. 9–10 MSG)

There you have it, dear ones. Since you asked, I say let's run loose and free, exactly as God encourages us to do.

OTHER SELECTIONS FOR WOMEN OF FAITH

Best-Selling authors and Women of Faith® speakers Patsy Clairmont, Mary Graham, Barbara Johnson, Marilyn Meberg, Grammy Award Winning singer Sandi Patty, Luci Swindoll, Sheila Walsh, Thelma Wells and dramatist Nicole Johnson bring humor and insight to women's daily lives. Sit back, exhale, and enjoy spending some time with these extraordinary women!

AVAILABLE WHEREVER BOOKS ARE SOLD.

THOMASNELSON.COM | WOMENOFFAITH.COM

W PUBLISHING GROUP
A Division of Thomas Nelson Publishers
Since 1798
wpublishinggroup.com

NELSON BOOKS
A Division of Thomas Nelson Publishers
Since 1798
thomasnelson.com

WOMEN OF FAITH
womenoffaith.com

COUNTRYMAN®
A Division of Thomas Nelson Publishers
Since 1798
thomasnelson.com

WOMEN OF FAITH®
Contagious JOY 2006

2006 EVENT CITIES & SPECIAL GUESTS

FEBRUARY 23-25
NATIONAL
FT. LAUDERDALE, FL
BankAtlantic Center

MARCH 31-APRIL 1
SHREVEPORT, LA
CenturyTel Center
*Avalon, Kathy Troccoli,
Anita Renfroe,
Donna VanLiere*

APRIL 7-8
HOUSTON, TX
Toyota Center
*Avalon, Max Lucado,
Chonda Pierce,
Donna VanLiere*

APRIL 21-22
SPOKANE, WA
Spokane Arena
*Avalon, Natalie Grant,
Anita Renfroe*

APRIL 28-29
COLUMBUS, OH
Nationwide Arena
*Natalie Grant,
Anita Renfroe,
Jennifer Rothschild*

JUNE 2-3
OMAHA, NE
Qwest Center
*Avalon, Anita Renfroe,
Tammy Trent,
Donna VanLiere*

JUNE 9-10
ROCHESTER, NY
Blue Cross Arena
*Avalon, Kathy Troccoli,
CeCe Winans,
Donna VanLiere*

JUNE 16-17
FRESNO, CA
SaveMart Center*
*Avalon, Natalie Grant,
Max Lucado,
Donna VanLiere*

JUNE 23-24
ATLANTA, GA
Philips Arena
*Avalon,
Nichole Nordeman,
Sherri Shepherd,
Donna VanLiere*

JULY 7-8
CHICAGO, IL
United Center
*Avalon,
Anita Renfroe,
CeCe Winans*

JULY 14-15
CLEVELAND, OH
Quicken Loans Arena
*Avalon, Natalie Grant,
Sherri Shepherd*

JULY 21-22
WASHINGTON, DC
MCI Center
*Avalon, Chonda Pierce,
Sherri Shepherd*

JULY 28-29
CALGARY, ALBERTA
Pengrowth Saddledome*
*Avalon, Carried Away,
Max Lucado,
Donna VanLiere*

AUGUST 4-5
ST. LOUIS, MO
Savvis Center
*Natalie Grant,
Anita Renfroe,
Sherri Shepherd,
Donna VanLiere*

AUGUST 11-12
HARTFORD, CT
Hartford Civic Center
*Avalon, Carol Kent,
Jennifer Rothschild*

AUGUST 18-19
FT. WAYNE, IN
War Memorial Coliseum
*Avalon, Natalie Grant,
Carol Kent*

AUGUST 25-26
DALLAS, TX
American Airlines Center
*Max Lucado,
Natalie Grant,
Robin McGraw*

SEPTEMBER 8-9
ANAHEIM, CA
Arrowhead Pond
*Avalon, Robin McGraw,
Jennifer Rothschild*

SEPTEMBER 15-16
PHILADELPHIA, PA
Wachovia Center
*Avalon, Robin McGraw,
Nicole C. Mullen*

SEPTEMBER 22-23
DENVER, CO
Pepsi Center
*Max Lucado,
Chonda Pierce,
Kathy Troccoli*

SEPTEMBER 29-30
SACRAMENTO, CA
ARCO Arena
*Avalon, Robin McGraw,
Nichole Nordeman*

OCTOBER 6-7
OKLAHOMA CITY, OK
Ford Center
*Avalon, Max Lucado,
Jennifer Rothschild,
Donna VanLiere*

OCTOBER 13-14
PORTLAND, OR
Rose Garden Arena
*Avalon, Carol Kent,
Kathy Troccoli,
Donna VanLiere*

OCTOBER 20-21
ST. PAUL, MN
Xcel Energy Center
*Avalon, Carol Kent,
Anita Renfroe*

OCTOBER 27-28
CHARLOTTE, NC
Charlotte Arena
*Avalon, Chonda Pierce,
Jennifer Rothschild*

NOVEMBER 3-4
VANCOUVER, BC
GM Place*
*Avalon, Carried Away,
Nichole Nordeman,
Donna VanLiere*

NOVEMBER 10-11
ORLANDO, FL
TD Waterhouse Centre
*Avalon,
Nicole C. Mullen,
Anita Renfroe,
Donna VanLiere*

NOVEMBER 17-18
PHOENIX, AZ
Glendale Arena*
*Avalon,
Nichole Nordeman,
Kathy Troccoli,
Donna VanLiere*

1-888-49-FAITH womenoffaith.com
*No Pre-Conference available. Dates, times, locations and special guests subject to change.
Visit womenoffaith.com for details on special guests, registration deadlines and pricing.